Real Money, Real Power?

Daniel Williams · Don Waisanen

Real Money, Real Power?

The Challenges with Participatory Budgeting in New York City

palgrave
macmillan

Daniel Williams
Marxe School of Public and
International Affairs
Baruch College
New York, NY, USA

Don Waisanen
Marxe School of Public and
International Affairs
Baruch College
New York, NY, USA

ISBN 978-3-030-59200-4   ISBN 978-3-030-59201-1 (eBook)
https://doi.org/10.1007/978-3-030-59201-1

This Palgrave Macmillan imprint is published by the registered company Springer Nature Switzerland AG
The registered company address is: Gewerbestrasse 11, 6330 Cham, Switzerland

Acknowledgments

We would like to thank the Howard J. Samuels State and City Policy Center at the Austin W. Marxe School of Public and International Affairs for its generous grant that allowed us to conduct the research reported here. We'd also like to thank our graduate research assistants, Marc Boyd, Ken Silverman, and Shana Kieran-Kaufman, for their contributions to this project; Rita Ormsby for bringing participatory budgeting to our attention many years ago; and our family, friends, and colleagues for all their support.

Contents

List of Figures

List of Tables

CHAPTER 1

Introduction

Abstract The introduction begins by recounting an evening observing a neighborhood assembly in Manhattan, introducing the point of early participatory budgeting (PB) as contrasted with clientelistic practices. We focus on what it's like to navigate the participatory budgeting process in the role of a regular community member, unconnected to a council member's office. We outline our hope that this book can help participatory budgeting reach its potential in serving citizens everywhere, advancing greater civic interest in and deliberative agency over allocations of taxpayer monies

Keywords Participatory budgeting · Clientelism · Deliberation, civic engagement · Public participation

Real Money, Real Power?

On a chilly September day, Dan went to a community center in Harlem to meet his graduate assistant (GA) for their first observation of a Participatory Budgeting Neighborhood Assembly. As he exited the subway and walked down a crowded New York City sidewalk a few minutes before the scheduled meeting, he received a text message from the GA advising that he might have difficulty finding the meeting. The advertised avenue address was not the entrance, so Dan would need to go to the side street

D. Williams and D. Waisanen, *Real Money, Real Power?*,
https://doi.org/10.1007/978-3-030-59201-1_1

and enter from the third door on the right. While passing the avenue side of the community center, he noticed a large participatory budgeting (PB) poster in the window, but no posted directions on how to get in.

Dan looked at his watch. He had blocked off plenty of time to attend the meeting yet was flustered at the possibility that he might be late. Following the GA's directions, he found a room with three staff but, strangely, no members of the public. The two researchers briefly chatted with the staffers, who, it then became clear, were a council staff member, an intern, and the community center director, who was serving the public by providing this space but was not there to take part in the meeting.

After a while four people arrived, two together. The council staffer began the meeting by attempting to play a video supplied for the introduction to participatory budgeting. The equipment didn't work, however. So the staffer provided his own, alternative introduction, including background on PB and a brief explanation of the type of local community project that might be eligible for citizens to vote on. He then asked for proposed projects. Only one was proposed. Two of the attendees indicated an interest in being delegates at the next, second-level meetings where the ballot is produced. It had been 32 minutes since the first constituent had arrived, the meeting was over.

This is democracy according to PB. Far from the well-orchestrated, well-attended, expansive effort at creating an inclusive and transparent form of budgeting espoused in so much of its messaging, for local citizens navigating PB can be a confusing hodgepodge of information and events, generating limited ideas, rushed meetings, and ultimately gamed by the usual suspects. Far from the ideals of a deliberative democracy, a lack of uniformity in scheduling, meeting designs, and other processes, in particular, seriously undermines the potential for citizens to have a voice in budget allocations.

The website for New York City's participatory budgeting project (PBNYC) has, for many years, featured a video that begins with the headline: "Real Money, Real Power." D. W. Williams, Calabrese, Gupta, and Harju (2017) show that the label "Real Money" is highly suspect from the outset, as the amount of the New York City capital budget committed to participatory budgeting is approximately 0.1% of the annual capital commitment. Participatory budgeting promotional materials assert that "Real Power" is exerted by "Real People." We understand real power to refer to the origin story of participatory budgeting (PB) in Porto Alegre,

Brazil, where, prior to reforms in the 1980s, the budget was substantially influenced, if not dominated, by clientelism. By clientelism, we mean the corrupt, corrupt-like,[1] or merely unmeritorious use of governmental funds to satisfy important constituents, rather than to use the resources for general public benefit.

As Plunkitt and Riordon (1905) discuss, clientelism can be attained through raiding the public trough while using a small portion of the windfall to provide a small measure of services to constituents to generate recurrent electoral success. However, in modern times, such overt graft is generally illegal and typically avoided. Earmarks,[2] also labeled "pork" (Maxey, 1919, p. 691), provide a work-around. Pork refers to the use of unmeritorious earmarks that are beneficial to individual legislators for political reasons, but are not beneficial to the general public (hence, "unmeritorious"). The link between earmarks and clientelism and their implicitly negative relation with real power creates a special concern for participatory budgeting in some of its forms. In particular, participatory budgeting in both Chicago and New York City has been implemented by the local legislative body through the use of earmarks controlled by individual council members.[3] Pin (2017) has shown that when a Chicago council member became displeased with some aspect of PB, decision power was withdrawn from PB participants.

As Calabrese, D. W. Williams, and Gupta (2020) show, it is likely that New York City Council members follow the advice of PB participants by distributing their discretionary funding (earmarks) to a larger number of smaller projects than other, non-engaged council members.[4] While

[1] By "corrupt-like," we intend practices that are not actually illegal, but might nevertheless be considered improper in common discourse.

[2] State and local governments use a variety of terms to refer to earmarks, consequently one must know the local culture to identify earmarks in particular budgets. For example, in New York City, they are commonly labeled "member items" and more formally referred to as "discretionary" expenditures. In New York State, they are labeled "community projects." It is entirely possible that these legislators also direct (earmark) other specific expenditures.

[3] In some jurisdictions, participatory budgeting is implemented through a central authority.

[4] This effect might be an artifact of the restrictions placed on PB by many council members. They set a target of $1 million to fund through participatory budgeting. For the participants to select several projects, they are, necessarily, small.

this can reflect dispersion of power, it may alternatively enact well-honed clientelism.

In this light, this book examines previously unexplored elements of the PBNYC project. While there has been substantial study of PBNYC (Castillo, 2015; Gilman, 2012, 2016; Hagelskamp, Rinehart, Silliman, & Schleifer, 2016; Kasdan & Cattell, 2012a, 2012b; Kasdan, Cattell, & Convey, 2013; Kasdan & Markman, 2017; Kasdan, Markman, & Convey, 2014; Mayorga, 2014; Pape & Lerner, 2016; Shybalkina & Bifulco, 2019; Su, 2012, 2017a, 2017b, 2018; Urban Justice Center, 2015), there has been a limited examination of what it's like for citizens to navigate the PB process, at the level of everyday life. As scholars concerned with maximizing citizens' capacities to engage in democratic processes (see also Waisanen, 2012, 2014, 2018, 2020), we set our sights on what it's like to interact with PB across a full annual cycle.

In the 2018–2019 budget preparation cycle for fiscal year 2020, 33 of 51 New York City council districts engaged in the PB process, with each districts' prior year engagement ranging from zero to seven cycles. The PB process involves various stages: idea generation, budget delegate meetings, expos, voting, and celebration. To critically examine top-down assertions about the real money and real power at play throughout this process, we sought to replicate citizens' experiences with PB across districts from the ground up, collecting multiple forms of data through all of these stages except the last (the delegate stage, in which participants refine the wide array of initial proposals to those that ultimately appear on the community ballots, was mostly closed to observers).

We attempted to view what it would be like for a local community member to navigate these processes, from a number of vantage points. From September 2018 through April 2019 the principal investigator and two research assistants conducted a variety of data gathering activities. After determining that there is no central information source on council member participatory budgeting activities, we contacted all 51 council district offices to identify opportunities to observe neighborhood assemblies. We attended seven neighborhood assemblies in Manhattan (three assemblies in three council districts), Brooklyn (one assembly/council district), and Queens (three assemblies in one council district). The research assistants each attended one budget delegate training session. At this point, a council office declared delegate meetings to be closed (a remarkable finding in and of itself—why would a participatory, taxpayer-funded process of any kind be deemed closed to the public!), so we paused data gathering while revising our Human Subjects application to account for this fact. After the revision, that council office refused further access. A second council district allowed access, but provided limited scheduling information, so we ultimately attended only one additional delegate session. To adjust for these limitations, we gathered data from online media (1295 observations), and various council communications including online and paper material from council offices (219 observations), and council member Facebook and Twitter feeds (78 data files, each of which contained numerous observations). Later, when the participatory budgeting process reached the voting stage, we conducted 12 pre-voting interviews at project expos and 66 post-voting interviews at pop-up voting locations, for a total 78 interviews distributed across Brooklyn, Queens, and Manhattan. All of these observations were conducted to see what citizens face when navigating PB.

To examine PBNYC's main claim, at every step we asked: "do citizens have real money and real power in participatory budgeting?" Contrary to the espoused influence of local people to determine city budget allocations across NYC, this project reports on the existence of clientelism, interest groups, expert influence, the limited voice and power of the marginalized, and a lack of transparency in too much of the participatory budgeting process. We also find that there is no singular Participatory Budgeting Project in New York City. Instead, there are numerous participatory budget projects, as many as there are council members who engage in the practice. Focusing especially on the fissures between PB's ideals and realities, we ultimately recommend that PB undergo substantial reforms.

To be clear, despite the wealth of evidence gathered, in this book we are not merely engaging in criticism for criticism's sake. We think that PB is a wonderful idea and well worth the investment and time that have been put into the initiative, in its different forms across the world. To truly reach the ideals of democracy and citizenship aspired to in so many jurisdictions, decisions about budgeting shouldn't be left to representatives and technocrats alone. To realize these ideals, however, simply getting excited about this novel enterprise and doing all possible to gloss over its problems does not serve the public interest. To this point, PB is almost wholly celebrated by practitioners and looked upon positively in much of the extant literature on the topic. On the other hand, we look to contribute to and realistically assess what emerges from the lived experience of navigating PB from the citizen's perspective, ultimately with the goal of improving its features and functions.

Our hope is that this book can further help PB reach its potential in serving citizens everywhere, advancing greater civic interest in and deliberative agency over allocations of taxpayer monies. Before diving further into this project's details, the next chapter provides some brief background and context for participatory democracy and specific developments related to participatory budgeting, which are necessary to understand how these processes came to be and what we know about them to this point.

References

Calabrese, T., Williams, D. W., & Gupta, A. (2020). Does participatory budgeting alter public spending? Evidence from New York City. *Administration and Society, 52*(9), 1382–1409. https://doi.org/10.1177/0095399720912548.

Castillo, M. (2015). Reflections on participatory budgeting in New York City. *The Innovation Journal: the Public Sector Innovation Journal, 20*(2), 1–11.

Gilman, H. R. (2012). Transformative deliberations: Participatory budgeting in the United States. *Journal of Public Deliberation, 8*(2) (Online).

Gilman, H. R. (2016). *Engaging citizens: Participatory budgeting and the inclusive governance movement within the United States*. Retrieved from http://ash.harvard.edu/files/ash/files/participatory-budgeting-paper.pdf?m=1455295224.

Hagelskamp, C., Rinehart, C., Silliman, R., & Schleifer, D. (2016). *Why let the people decide? Elected officials on participatory budgeting*. Retrieved from https://www.publicagenda.org/files/WhyLetThePeopleDecide_PublicAgenda_2016.pdf.

Kasdan, A., & Cattell, L. (2012a). *A people's budget: A research and evaluation report on the pilot year of participatory budgeting in New York City*. Retrieved from https://cdp.urbanjustice.org/sites/default/files/pbreport.pdf.

Kasdan, A., & Cattell, L. (2012b). *A people's budget: A research and evaluation report on the pilot year of participatory budgeting in New York City*. Retrieved from https://www.issuelab.org/resource/a-people-s-budget-a-research-and-evaluation-report-on-the-pilot-year-of-participatory-budgeting-in-new-york-city.html.

Kasdan, A., Cattell, L., & Convey, P. (2013). *A people's budget: A research and evaluation report on participatory budgeting in New York City—Year 2*. Retrieved from https://cdp.urbanjustice.org/sites/default/files/pbreport_year2_0.pdf.

Kasdan, A., & Markman, E. (2017). Participatory budgeting and community-based research: Principles, practices, and implications for impact validity. *New Political Science, 39*(1), 143–155.

Kasdan, A., Markman, E., & Convey, P. (2014). *A people's budget: A research and evaluation report on participatory budgeting in New York City—Year 3*. Retrieved from https://cdp.urbanjustice.org/sites/default/files/CDP.WEB.doc_Report_PBNYC-cycle3-FullReport_20141030.pdf.

Maxey, C. C. (1919). A little history of pork. *National Municipal Review, 8*(10), 691–705. https://doi.org/10.1002/ncr.4110081006.

Mayorga, E. (2014). Toward digital, critical, participatory action research: Lessons from the #BarrioEdProj. *The Journal of Interactive Technology & Pedagogy, 5*. 1–25. https://jitp.commons.gc.cuny.edu/toward-digital-critical-participatory-action-research/.

Pape, M., & Lerner, J. (2016). Budgeting for equity: How can participatory budgeting advance equity in the United States? *Journal of Public Deliberation, 12*(2), Article 9.

Pin, L. (2017). Does participatory budgeting lead to local empowerment? The case of Chicago, IL. *Alternate Routes: A Journal of Critical Social Research, 28*.

Plunkitt, G. W., & Riordon, W. L. (1905). *Plunkitt of Tammany Hall: A series of very plain talks on very practical politics*. New York: McClure, Phillips & Co.

Shybalkina, I., & Bifulco, R. (2019). Does participatory budgeting change the share of public funding to low income neighborhoods? *Public Budgeting & Finance, 39*(1), 45–66. https://doi.org/10.1111/pbaf.12212.

Su, C. (2012). Whose budget? Our budget? Broadening political stakeholdership via participatory budgeting. *Journal of Public Deliberation, 8*(2), Article 1.

Su, C. (2017a). *Beyond inclusion: Critical race theory and participatory budgeting*. CUNY Academic Works. Retrieved from http://academicworks.cuny.edu/gc_pubs/299.

Su, C. (2017b). *From Porto Alegre to New York City: Participatory budgeting and democracy*. CUNY Academic Works. City University of New York (CUNY). Retrieved from http://academicworks.cuny.edu/gc_pubs/305.

Su, C. (2018). Managed participation: City agencies and micropolitics in participatory budgeting. *Nonprofit and Voluntary Sector Quarterly, 47*(4_Suppl.), 76S–96S. https://doi.org/10.1177/0899764018757029.

Urban Justice Center. (2015). *A people's budget: A research and evaluation report on participatory budgeting in New York City—Cycle 4 key research findings*. Retrieved from https://cdp.urbanjustice.org/sites/default/files/CDP.WEB.doc_Report_PBNYC_cycle4findings_20151021.pdf.

Waisanen, D. (2012). Bordering populism in immigration activism: Outlaw–civic discourse in a (counter) public. *Communication Monographs, 79*, 232–255.

Waisanen, D. (2014). Toward robust public engagement: The value of deliberative discourse for civil communication. *Rhetoric & Public Affairs, 17*, 287–322.

Waisanen, D. (2018). *Political conversion: Personal transformation as strategic public communication*. Lexington Studies in Political Communication. Lanham, MD: Rowman & Littlefield.

Waisanen, D. (2020). *Improv for democracy: How to bridge differences and develop the communication and leadership skills our world needs*. New Political Science Series. Albany, NY: State University of New York Press.

Williams, D. W., Calabrese, T., Gupta, A., & Harju, S. (2017). *How does participatory budgeting affect council member priorities?* Paper presented at the Association of Budgeting & Financial Management Annual Conference, Washington.

CHAPTER 2

Participatory Budgeting from the Past to the Present

Abstract This chapter reviews the mid-twentieth century developments around participatory democracy as a precursor to participatory budgeting. It then introduces participatory budgeting in New York City and reviews the historical context of citizen budget participation through the community board process, which city agencies have taken over as a place to advocate for agency projects.

Keywords History · Community board · City agencies · Advocacy

In this chapter, we provide some important background and context for PB. Before exploring the nuances of PB in the present, it's critical to see the issues and tensions at play in past efforts to advance more and better forms of public participation, which each have relevance to this project.

The mid-twentieth century literature on participatory democracy emphasized education in democracy and citizenship (Hart, 1972; Pateman, 1970; Wolfe, 1985),[1] with extended literature focusing on how such processes legitimize governance (Alves & Allegretti, 2012; Fung, 2015; Goldfrank, 2012; Richard & David, 2018; Souza, 2001; Wampler, 2012). In this literature, there was until recently little focus on what

[1] Focusing on ballot initiatives, Dyck and Lascher (2019) dispute the view that participatory processes necessarily have an educative effect.

D. Williams and D. Waisanen, *Real Money, Real Power?*,
https://doi.org/10.1007/978-3-030-59201-1_2

budgets are or do: budgets are proposals (and processes) for decisions and they provide the means for making those decisions. Arnstein (1969) describes eight stages of participation on a continuum: citizen control, delegated power, partnership, placation, consultation, informing, therapy, and manipulation. If PBNYC is related to the reduction or elimination of clientelism, it should be near the pole of citizen control; however, if it is a mask for continued or enhanced clientelism, it may approach its opposite. To determine where in this progression PBNYC falls, it's essential to observe precisely how proposed projects are refined to become ballot options.

For PB to transfer control to citizens and residents, it is not enough to allow them to vote, they must be able to place items on the agenda for voting. It is well known that setting an agenda can be the most important stage of decision-making (McCombs & Shaw, 1993; Plott & Levine, 1978; Stone, 1980; Walker, 1977). For PB, this means placing proposals on the ballot. For PBNYC this placement arises through a multistage process, and it is this process that requires observation. To further understand these processes, some sense of both the background and types of PB that have emerged around the world proves useful, before delving into some historical and current perspectives on PB in NYC.

The Origin of Participatory Budgeting

PB emerged in Porto Alegre, Brazil in the late 1980s (Goldfrank, 2007). In the Brazilian version, residents allocate substantial budgetary shares in their local communities, frequently to achieve social justice goals. For example, Porto Alegre, Brazil committed as much as 21% of its municipal budget to participatory budgeting in the early 1990s (Souza, 2001). Belo Horizonte, Brazil committed 40% of their investment (capital) budget through the participatory budgeting process in 1994 (Paixão Bretas, 1996). In this initial run, community members allocated funds largely to sanitation and road paving.

Following this initial success, activities labeled PB have diffused to roughly 15 countries and more than 3000 cities, and continue to spread (Goldfrank, 2012; Su, 2017). PB's first implementation in North America was in Guelph, Canada beginning in 1999 (Pinnington, Lerner, & Schugurensky, 2009; Sintomer, Herzberg, Allegretti, Röcke, & Alves, 2013). An advocacy group brought participatory budgeting to Chicago beginning in 2009 (Hadden & Lerner, 2011).

The Participatory Budgeting Project (2018) reports that there have been over 310 participatory budgeting processes in North America during the last two decades, with many continuing into the most recent budget cycle. Many instances of North American and European Participatory Budgeting Projects substantially differ from the original Porto Alegre model, however (Lerner, 2011; Pateman, 2012; Patsias, Latendresse, & Bherer, 2013; Sintomer et al., 2013). Importantly, Patsias et al. (2013) characterize the European version as "consultative," "top-down," and "only very partially autonomous" (p. 2221).

Participatory Budgeting in NYC

In 2011, four New York City council members began allowing residents of their respective districts to select capital projects for funding from a portion of the member-directed discretionary capital funding for fiscal year 2013 (Participatory Budgeting in New York City, 2011). This process has continued, growing to 31 council members for fiscal 2019 (New York City Council, 2017).[2] During the early years, evaluations largely focused on demographics, process, and participant perceptions (Kasdan & Cattell, 2012; Kasdan, Cattell, & Convey, 2013; Kasdan, Markman, & Convey, 2014; Urban Justice Center, 2015).

Council members typically contribute $1 million of their $5 million discretionary capital allocation, thereby retaining substantial additional discretionary funding not committed to the process. For the early cycles, New York, like Chicago, restricted projects to capital projects, but members also have discretionary expense funds—and beginning in Cycle 8 for fiscal 2019, one member funded several expense projects (Wong, 2018). New York City allocates roughly 0.1% of its capital budget (16% of the council directed discretionary capital funding) through the participatory process (New York City, 2017)—critically, an entirely different scale than found in early Brazilian participatory budgeting.

[2] For the budget development for fiscal year 2020 (the time period of this research), 33 members' offices provided phone responses that they were engaged in PB during this cycle. In September 2018, a charter revision substantially changed PBNYC for development for fiscal years 2022 and later. The revision established a citizen engagement commission with a charge to create a citywide participatory budgeting process. This citywide process does not replace the council based process; the two will operate in parallel.

In PBNYC, participants suggest projects that might be funded. City officials determine whether these projects are eligible for funding and determine their expected cost. Volunteer budget delegates then refine the project list to a small number. These remaining projects, with costs attached, are offered to the participants who vote for their preferred projects. The selected projects are those that receive the most votes in rank order, until the allocated funds are exhausted (New York City Council, 2017; Participatory Budgeting Project, 2017).

Some Historical and Current Perspective for NYC

New York already had a general citizen budget participation process many years before the origination of participatory budgeting.[3] This process involves community boards, which have, as one of their functions, an annual budget request. The predecessors of the current community boards were community district planning boards, first established by the Manhattan Borough President in 1951 and expanded to all five boroughs in 1963 (Kihss, 1963). In the 1975 New York City Charter revisions, these became 59 community boards and their associated community districts (Pecorella, 1989). Unlike the 51 city council districts that change with census updates, the community districts have fixed borders. In the 2010 Census, their populations ranged from 51,000 to 241,000, with an average of 139,000 ("New York City Population by Community Districts," 2017). Borough presidents appoint community boards in consultation with council members.

Pecorella (1986, 1988, 1989, 1994) provides a mixed but mostly upbeat analysis of community board budgeting. He suggests that upper income white neighborhoods are more successful than other communities in obtaining funding for their capital budgets, while his reported data actually show relatively poor performance for communities in general. Although Pecorella says the data for the later period shows better performance than the earlier period,[4] most of his data show limited success.

[3] This section providing a historical perspective is substantially similar to a section that can be found in an unpublished working paper by D. W. Williams, Calabrese, Gupta, and Harju (2017).

[4] Pecorella (1989) shows that in 1985 the community boards achieved a 33% success rate for capital projects, which was an increase of 11 percentage points from 22% in 1982. Pecorella (1994) shows these figures as 50 and 36% respectively. The difference reflects

Any successes achieved appear to depend on agency cosponsorship; it is not clear who constitutes the actual primary requestor and the cosponsor. Pecorella points out that the 1989 charter revision weakened the community board role indirectly when it eliminated the Board of Estimate, because the borough presidents, who had appointed members to the Board of Estimate, lost a substantial role in the budget process. In fact, the current charter does not contain some of the strongest language in support of community board budgeting that Pecorella found in the 1975 charter revisions ("New York City Charter as Amended Through July 2004," 2004; Pecorella, 1994, pp. 151–152).

The community boards' budget activities include consultation with city agencies, development of a "Statement of Community District Needs" that is submitted to the New York City Office of Management and Budget (NYCOMB) and published by the Department of Planning, preparation of a budget request that includes a list of expense and capital budget items, conducting public hearings, and submitting the budget request to the NYCOMB ("Handbook for Community Board Members," 2014; "New York City Charter As Amended Through July 2004," 2004, §§ 230–231). Several of these activities were explicitly required in the 1975 charter (Pecorella, 1994), but are no longer part of the City Charter ("New York City Charter as Amended Through July 2004," 2004). The capital and expense budgets are collected together for all community boards in a massive document labeled the "budget register." A review of any recent budget register shows that the community boards are not always clear as to what counts as a capital versus expense budget item ("Register of Community Board Budget Requests For The Executive Budget Fiscal Year 2018," 2017).[5] This is remarkable given how ambiguous the funds for participatory budgeting may be to some people.

The register also shows a curious tendency for the same or similar requests to recur throughout. For example, the cited register requests funding for fire departments to provide smoke detectors eight times.[6] For

a different treatment of continued funding, which he excludes in 1989 since these can reflect projects that do not originate at the community boards. These success rates clearly do not match the promise of actual decisions as promised with participatory budgeting.

[5] This report, which is published multiple times a year for various stages of the budget, can be found at www1.nyc.gov/site/omb/publications/budget-reports.page?report=Comm%20Bd%20Register.

[6] There are also eight requests in the 2019 budget register for FY 2020.

over a decade, the fire department has brought its smoke detector request to the community boards every year. The proposal arises at the agency and is farmed out to community boards as a suggested proposal. This phenomenon results from the consultation process, which provides an opportunity for city agencies to lobby the representatives of the community boards to include their agency needs within the community board budget requests.[7]

By organizing these consultations in this format, the NYCOMB assists agencies in obtaining supplemental funding through community board processes, rather than assisting community boards to obtain additional information that would assist them in developing meaningful requests associated with local community needs. Considering this relatively weak performance of community board budgeting, the advent of participatory budgeting as a replacement process is not surprising.

The community board process is principally a borough president activity. Borough presidents are the chief executive officers of the five counties (called boroughs) that make up New York City. These offices were significantly disempowered by the 1989 charter revision, which was required in a Supreme Court Ruling ("Board of Estimate of NYC v. Morris, 489 U.S. 688," 1989) that eliminated the Board of Estimate because it provided unequal representation for residents of the five boroughs. As a consequence, borough presidents lost their roles for selecting a Board of Estimate member and, thereby, lost a significant role in budget making. The budget function of the community boards is advisory only. The participatory budgeting process is similar to the budget function of the community boards, but it has been organized by the city council and the promise made is that within the scope of valid projects, the decisions made will be honored so community members are authorized to make final decisions. It is within this overall context that current efforts at PB are nested and largely celebrated.

References

Alves, M. L., & Allegretti, G. (2012). (In)stability, a key element to understand participatory budgeting: Discussing Portuguese cases. *Journal of Public Deliberation, 8*(2), Article 3.

[7] An author of this project participated in this process for several years between 2007 and 2010.

Arnstein, S. R. (1969). A ladder of citizen participation. *Journal of the American Institute of Planners, 35*(4), 216–224.

Board of Estimate of NYC v. Morris, 489 U.S. 688 (1989).

Dyck, J. J., & Lascher, E. L. (2019). *Initiatives without engagement: A realistic appraisal of direct democracy's secondary effects*. Ann Arbor: University of Michigan Press.

Fung, A. (2015). Putting the public back into governance: The challenges of citizen participation and its future. *Public Administration Review, 75*(4), 513–522. https://doi.org/10.1111/puar.12361.

Goldfrank, B. (2007). Lessons from Latin American experience in participatory budgeting. In A. Shah (Ed.), *Participatory budgeting* (Vol. 143, pp. 91–126). Washington, DC: The World Bank.

Goldfrank, B. (2012). The World Bank and the globalization of participatory budgeting. *Journal of Public Deliberation, 8*(2), Article 7.

Hadden, M., & Lerner, J. (2011, December 7). *How to start participatory budgeting in Your City*. Retrieved from http://www.commondreams.org/views/2011/12/07/how-start-participatory-budgeting-your-city.

Handbook for Community Board Members. (2014). In New York City (Ed.): Office of the Mayor Community Affairs Unit.

Hart, D. K. (1972). Theories of government related to decentralization and citizen participation. *Public Administration Review, 32*, 603–621. https://doi.org/10.2307/975228.

Kasdan, A., & Cattell, L. (2012). *A people's budget: A research and evaluation report on the pilot year of participatory budgeting in New York City*. Retrieved from https://www.issuelab.org/resource/a-people-s-budget-a-research-and-evaluation-report-on-the-pilot-year-of-participatory-budgeting-in-new-york-city.html.

Kasdan, A., Cattell, L., & Convey, P. (2013). *A people's budget: A research and evaluation report on participatory budgeting in New York City—Year 2*. Retrieved from https://cdp.urbanjustice.org/sites/default/files/pbreport_year2_0.pdf.

Kasdan, A., Markman, E., & Convey, P. (2014). *A people's budget: A research and evaluation report on participatory budgeting in New York City—Year 3*. Retrieved from https://cdp.urbanjustice.org/sites/default/files/CDP.WEB.doc_Report_PBNYC-cycle3-FullReport_20141030.pdf.

Kihss, P. (1963, April 29). New city charter still under test: Changes are numerous as system is learned. *The New York Times*, p. 23.

Lerner, J. (2011). Participatory budgeting: Building community agreement around tough budget decisions. *National Civic Review, 100*(2), 30–35. https://doi.org/10.1002/ncr.20059.

McCombs, M. E., & Shaw, D. L. (1993). The evolution of agenda-setting research: Twenty-five years in the marketplace of ideas. *Journal of Communication, 43*(2), 58–67.

New York City. (2017). *Adopted Capital Budget For Fiscal Year 2018*. Retrieved from http://www1.nyc.gov/site/omb/publications/finplan06-17.page.

New York City Council. (2017). Rulebook 2017–2018 New York City participatory budgeting. In New York City Council (Ed.).

New York City Charter As Amended Through July 2004. (2004). Retrieved from www.nyc.gov/html/records/pdf/section%201133_citycharter.pdf accessible at http://www.amlegal.com/codes/client/new-york-city_ny/.

New York City Population by Community Districts. (2017). Retrieved from https://data.cityofnewyork.us/City-Government/New-York-City-Population-By-Community-Districts/xi7c-iiu2/data.

Paixão Bretas, P. R. (1996). Participative budgeting in Belo Horizonte: Democratization and citizenship. *Environment and Urbanization, 8*(1), 213–222.

Participatory Budgeting in New York City. (2011). *2011–2012 Handbook*.

Participatory Budgeting Project. (2017). *Participatory Budgeting Project*. Retrieved from https://www.participatorybudgeting.org/.

Participatory Budgeting Project. (2018). *PB map & process list*. Retrieved from https://www.participatorybudgeting.org/pb-map/.

Pateman, C. (1970). *Participation and democratic theory*. Cambridge, UK: University Press.

Pateman, C. (2012). APSA presidential address: Participatory democracy revisited. *Perspectives on Politics, 10*(1), 7–19.

Patsias, C., Latendresse, A., & Bherer, L. (2013). Participatory democracy, decentralization and local governance: The Montreal Participatory Budget in the light of 'empowered participatory governance'. *International Journal of Urban and Regional Research, 37*(6), 2214–2230. https://doi.org/10.1111/j.1468-2427.2012.01171.x.

Pecorella, R. F. (1986). Community input and the city budget: Geographically based budgeting in New York City. *Journal of Urban Affairs, 8*(1), 57–70.

Pecorella, R. F. (1988). Community empowerment revisited: Two decades of integrative reform. *State & Local Government Review, 20*(2), 72–78.

Pecorella, R. F. (1989). Community governance: A decade of experience. *Proceedings of the Academy of Political Science, 37*(3), 97–109. https://doi.org/10.2307/1173755.

Pecorella, R. F. (1994). *Community power in a postreform city: Politics in New York City*. Armonk: ME Sharpe.

Pinnington, E., Lerner, J., & Schugurensky, D. (2009). Participatory budgeting in North America: The case of Guelph, Canada. *Journal of Public Budgeting, Accounting & Financial Management, 21*(3), 454–481.

Plott, C. R., & Levine, M. E. (1978). A model of agenda influence on committee decisions. *The American Economic Review, 68*(1), 146–160.

Register of Community Board Budget Requests for the Executive Budget Fiscal Year 2018. (2017). Retrieved from http://www1.nyc.gov/assets/omb/downloads/pdf/cbrboro4-17.pdf.

Richard, E., & David, L. F. (2018). The future of citizen engagement in cities—The council of citizen engagement in sustainable urban strategies (ConCensus). *Futures, 101,* 80–91. https://doi.org/10.1016/j.futures.2018.06.012.

Sintomer, Y., Herzberg, C., Allegretti, G., Röcke, A., & Alves, M. L. (2013). *Participatory budgeting worldwide*. Retrieved from https://estudogeral.sib.uc.pt/jspui/bitstream/10316/42267/1/Participatory%20Budgeting%20Worldwide.pdf.

Souza, C. (2001). Participatory budgeting in Brazilian cities: Limits and possibilities in building democratic institutions. *Environment and Urbanization, 13*(1), 159–184. https://doi.org/10.1177/095624780101300112.

Stone, C. N. (1980). Systemic power in community decision making: A restatement of stratification theory. *American Political Science Review, 74*(4), 978–990.

Su, C. (2017b). *From Porto Alegre to New York City: Participatory budgeting and democracy*. CUNY Academic Works. City University of New York (CUNY). Retrieved from http://academicworks.cuny.edu/gc_pubs/305.

Urban Justice Center. (2015). *A people's budget: A research and evaluation report on participatory budgeting in New York City—Cycle 4 key research findings*. Retrieved from https://cdp.urbanjustice.org/sites/default/files/CDP.WEB.doc_Report_PBNYC_cycle4findings_20151021.pdf.

Walker, J. L. (1977). Setting the agenda in the US Senate: A theory of problem selection. *British Journal of Political Science, 7*(4), 423–445.

Wampler, B. (2012). Participatory budgeting: Core principles and key impacts. *Journal of Public Deliberation, 8*(2), Article 12.

Williams, D. W., Calabrese, T., Gupta, A., & Harju, S. (2017). *How does participatory budgeting affect council member priorities?* Paper presented at the Association of Budgeting & Financial Management Annual Conference, Washington.

Wolfe, J. D. (1985). A defense of participatory democracy. *The Review of Politics, 47*(3), 370–389.

Wong, P. (2018, May 1). District 39 participatory budgeting 2018: Winning projects announced. *Bklyner* (Online). Retrieved from https://bklyner.com/district-39-participatory-budgeting-2018-winning-projects-announced/.

CHAPTER 3

Between Policy Promises and Program Implementation

Abstract This chapter raises a concern about participatory budgeting in New York City (PBNYC): in the implementation stage, the city council member is also the program administrator, leading to many of the concerns that this book raises. We detail the theoretical constructs of power, clientelism, interest groups, and the possible role of experts in determining if citizens have real money and real power.

Keywords Implementation · Power · Clientalism · Interest groups

As Pressman and Wildavsky (1973) found almost 50 years ago, a program's promise and design can falter at the implementation stage. Most implementation literature from then to now focuses on the bureaucratic implementation of policies that are, at least nominally, made by a separate legislative body. This reflects the "steering" vs "rowing" metaphor later used in the reinventing government literature (Osborne & Gaebler, 1992) as a nudge for privatization, but removed one step, with the legislature steering and the governmental agent rowing. Pressman and Wildavsky suggest that there actually needs to be a much closer relationship between the two, with the policy maker remaining engaged during the implementation stage.

More recent literature continues to treat the role of the policy champion as important (Hendy & Barlow, 2012; McTigue, Rye, & Monios,

D. Williams and D. Waisanen, *Real Money, Real Power?*,
https://doi.org/10.1007/978-3-030-59201-1_3

2018). Yet, what if the policy maker not only steers, but also rows? How is this related to implementation? With the New York City model of participatory budgeting, implementation is never handed off to the bureaucracy; instead it is made part of the legislative office's function. Can we treat this as a policy or does it remain a political activity? For this project, the following integrates the literature with a set of research topics, looking between the ideal policy promises and the real program implementation of initiatives like participatory budgeting. These themes form a foundation for each of the multiple angles and approaches we take with PBNYC. The methods used in this study are addressed in context in the discussion and summarized in Appendix A.

What Primary Implementation Issues Does PB Focus?

To examine this form of implementation in PBNYC, we turn to four concepts that the existence of these processes underscore. Given their important roles for our research design, we conducted this project with each of them in mind.

Power

The overt claim underlying participatory budgeting is that it provides "real power" over "real money" for "real people," as we've described. We can discount the claim of real money, as PB's relative share of the New York City capital budget is 0.1%. As the capital budget is approximately one half the size of the expense budget, PB's net share of the total annual expenditure plan is 0.03%. While the gross sum of money, $1 million per council district, sounds like real money, in the context of New York City's overall budget, it's not.

For "real power" we look to meaningful decision-making, similar to what was found in Brazil in the 1990s (Paixão Bretas, 1996; Souza, 2001). Voting seems important, but what is more important is setting the agenda (McCombs & Shaw, 1993; Plott & Levine, 1978; Stone, 1980; Walker, 1977) by deciding what is on the ballot. For PB, deciding what to vote about involves several steps: suggesting items in person at meetings, through media such as idea cards, or through an online idea map—this stage is open to everyone interested; validating these items as eligible and clarifying them enough to make them genuine projects—these stages are shared between volunteer budget delegates, a district participatory budget committee, council staff, and agency personnel; designating a cost for the project (which is managed by agency personnel); and winnowing the set to a manageable number for a ballot, also performed by the delegates and district committee. The steps between validating and winnowing can be iterative.

The term "real people" is vague, so to define it we have looked first to the South American roots of participatory budgeting where substantial resources were redirected from privileged communities to those in need. In early evaluation reports of PBNYC completed by a sponsoring organization, there are assertions such as, "A higher percentage of African Americans participated in neighborhood assemblies (30%), compared to the full population in the eight districts (17%)" (Kasdan et al., 2013, p. 16) and "21% of budget delegates and 19% of PB voters were born outside of the United States" (Kasdan & Cattell, 2012, p. 18). It was also reported that "1 out of 3 neighborhood assembly participants and budget delegates and 44% of PB voters had never worked with others in their community to solve a problem before PB" (Kasdan & Cattell, 2012, p. 18). There are numerous other, similar assertions, which are provided as evidence that PB is doing what's expected. Thus, we conclude that "real people" refers to the underrepresented, under-engaged, and generally underserved population. As mentioned, the purpose of this project is, quite simply, to see if and how such real people have real power.

Clientelism

It is frequently argued that participatory budgeting exists to negate clientelistic (patronage) practices (Alves, 1990; Assies, 1993; Avritzer, 2010; Bremner, 1998; Wampler, McNulty, & Touchton, 2018). However, there is some evidence that clientelism might be compatible with instantiations of participatory budgeting (Pin, 2017; Wampler & Touchton, 2016). In New York City, voluntarily engaged council members use part of their discretionary funds—funds that exist as a legal form of patronage—to fund participatory budgeting. Thus, we anticipated that we might find evidence that PBNYC will reflect, rather than negate, clientelistic practices.

Interest Groups

Early participatory democracy literature distinguished between participatory practices that focus on the well-being of the population as a whole (frequently using the Rousseauian term, “general will”) and Schumpeterian pluralism focused on defending individual interests (Macpherson, 1980; Pateman, 1975). Yet, there is extensive discussion of coalitions—civil society, new grassroots organizations, etc.—within participatory budgeting (de Sousa Santos, 1998; Souza, 2001; Wampler & Avritzer, 2004). These organizations may sometimes act as interest groups (Wan, 2018). PBNYC was originally organized through the joint effort of council members and civil society groups, although the relationship between these two groups changed with the selection of the most recent previous Speaker of the Council, who was one of the original PB sponsoring council members. Nevertheless, there may be continuing involvement of civil society or new, less formal, groups, or even hidden and offline networks of influence (See Van Duyn, 2018). These groups may contribute to the participatory, democratic well-being of the whole, or they may act as interest groups through such practices as lobbying, which may appear as efforts by advocates to convince others, such as budget delegates or voters, to select their projects; agenda management, which may appear as the use of influence to receive preferential treatment, particularly at the stage of selecting items to appear on participatory budgeting ballots; and vote trading, which can appear in ballot making, where two (or more) sets of advocates agree to support each other’s projects for inclusion on the ballot, and can also appear in the voting process where supporters of two (or more) projects can agree to vote for each other’s projects. These are open questions that require critical insight.

Experts

In the context of participatory budgeting, experts may not always perceive themselves to be experts, but they may bring specific expert information and values into decision-making. Goodsell (2004) argues that the only significant way that governmental experts differ from the population at large is that they overvalue their own programs in comparison with everyone else. As an example, teachers may bring information about classrooms and more highly value education objectives, while thinking of themselves as community members.

Government by expert is part of what participatory practices aim to overcome (Fung, 2006). Yet the desired role of experts is ambiguous and may reflect an expectation of subservience (Baiocchi & Ganuza, 2014) or some form of joint engagement (Fung & Wright, 2001). An expectation for our research was that experts would be observed and that the role they play could be better understood relative to the question of whether citizens receive real money and real power.

With this background and these implementation issues in mind, we next turn to our research design, methodology, and the first round of observations from this research. Seeing distributions of money and power in action, our most prominent finding concerned a lack of transparency encountered in the citizen experience of PB. We'll outline many of the challenges associated with these findings and for the future of PB.

References

Alves, M. H. M. (1990, September). Building democratic socialism: The Partido Dos Trabalhadores in Brazil. *Monthly Review, 42,* 1+ (Online).

Assies, W. (1993). Urban social movements and local democracy in Brazil. *Revista Europea de Estudios Latinoamericanos y del Caribe/European Review of Latin American and Caribbean Studies* (55), 39–58.

Avritzer, L. (2010). Living under a democracy: Participation and its impact on the living conditions of the poor. *Latin American Research Review, 45,* 166–185.

Baiocchi, G., & Ganuza, E. (2014). Participatory budgeting as if emancipation mattered. *Politics & Society, 42*(1), 29–50. https://doi.org/10.1177/0032329213512978.

Bremner, L. (1998). Participatory planning. *Urban Forum, 9*(1), 111–119.

de Sousa Santos, B. (1998). Participatory budgeting in Porto Alegre: Toward a redistributive democracy. *Politics and Society, 26*(4), 461–510.

Fung, A. (2006). Varieties of participation in complex governance. *Public Administration Review, 66,* 66–75.

Fung, A., & Wright, E. O. (2001). Deepening democracy: Innovations in empowered participatory governance. *Politics & Society, 29*(1), 5–41.

Goodsell, C. T. (2004). *The case for bureaucracy: A public administration polemic* (4th ed.). Washington, DC: CQ Press.

Hendy, J., & Barlow, J. (2012). The role of the organizational champion in achieving health system change. *Social Science & Medicine, 74*(3), 348–355.

Kasdan, A., & Cattell, L. (2012). *A people's budget: A research and evaluation report on the pilot year of participatory budgeting in New York City*. Retrieved from https://cdp.urbanjustice.org/sites/default/files/pbreport.pdf.

Kasdan, A., Cattell, L., & Convey, P. (2013). *A people's budget: A research and evaluation report on participatory budgeting in New York City—Year 2*. Retrieved from https://cdp.urbanjustice.org/sites/default/files/pbreport_year2_0.pdf.

Macpherson, C. B. (1980). Pluralism, individualism, and participation. *Economic and Industrial Democracy, 1*(1), 21–30.

McCombs, M. E., & Shaw, D. L. (1993). The evolution of agenda-setting research: Twenty-five years in the marketplace of ideas. *Journal of Communication, 43*(2), 58–67.

McTigue, C., Rye, T., & Monios, J. (2018). The role of reporting mechanisms in transport policy implementation by local authorities in England. *Case Studies on Transport Policy, 6*(3), 319–328.

Osborne, D., & Gaebler, T. (1992). *Reinventing government: How the entrepreneurial spirit is transforming the public sector*. Reading, MA: Addison-Wesley.

Paixão Bretas, P. R. (1996). Participative budgeting in Belo Horizonte: Democratization and citizenship. *Environment and Urbanization, 8*(1), 213–222.

Pateman, C. (1975). A contribution to the political theory of organizational democracy. *Administration & Society, 7*(1), 5–26.

Pin, L. (2017). Does participatory budgeting lead to local empowerment? The case of Chicago, IL. *Alternate Routes: A Journal of Critical Social Research, 28*.

Plott, C. R., & Levine, M. E. (1978). A model of agenda influence on committee decisions. *The American Economic Review, 68*(1), 146–160.

Pressman, J. L., & Wildavsky, A. B. (1973). *Implementation: How great expectations in Washington are dashed in Oakland; or, Why it's amazing that Federal programs work at all, this being a saga of the Economic Development Administration as told by two sympathetic observers who seek to build morals on a foundation of ruined hopes*. Berkeley: University of California Press.

Souza, C. (2001). Participatory budgeting in Brazilian cities: Limits and possibilities in building democratic institutions. *Environment and Urbanization, 13*(1), 159–184. https://doi.org/10.1177/095624780101300112.

Stone, C. N. (1980). Systemic power in community decision making: A restatement of stratification theory. *American Political Science Review, 74*(4), 978–990.

Van Duyn, Emily. (2018). Hidden democracy: Political dissent in rural America. *Journal of Communication, 68*(5), 965–987.

Walker, J. L. (1977). Setting the agenda in the US Senate: A theory of problem selection. *British Journal of Political Science, 7*(4), 423–445.

Wampler, B., & Avritzer, L. (2004). Participatory publics: Civil society and new institutions in democratic Brazil. *Comparative Politics, 36*(3), 291–312. https://doi.org/10.2307/4150132.

Wampler, B., & Touchton, M. (2016). Public engagement for public health: Participatory budgeting and infant mortality in Brazilian municipalities. In W. No, A. Brennan, & D. Schugurensky (Eds.), *By the people* (pp. 144–154). Phoenix, AZ: Arizona State University.

Wampler, B., McNulty, S., & Touchton, M. (2018). *Participatory budgeting: Spreading across the globe.* Retrieved from http://www.transparency-initiative.org/wp-content/uploads/2018/03/spreading-pb-across-the-globe_jan-2018.pdf.

Wan, P. Y.-Z. (2018). Outsourcing participatory democracy: Critical reflections on the participatory budgeting experiences in Taiwan. *Journal of Public Deliberation, 14*(1), 7.

CHAPTER 4

The Challenges of Neighborhood Assemblies

Abstract This chapter details observations related to attending idea-generating events labeled "neighborhood assemblies" conducted by council member offices in the late summer and fall of a PB annual cycle. We raise concerns about the difficulty in obtaining access for the ordinary community member, the lack of a centralized process or central information source (including a lack of transparency in meeting posting and design), the lack of a consistent process between council districts (and the variability of meeting experiences), the overrepresentation by governmental representatives as participants (ultimately demonstrating the limited ideas generated through the top-down involvement of various actors and agencies), and a lack of cooperation from governmental agencies.

Keywords Neighborhood assemblies, access · Transparency · Representative

By design, our research team approached observation as members of the public. We wanted to get as close to the citizen experience of PB as possible, without presuming to know what many of these processes would be like, at least from the outset. Some published research on participatory budgeting reflects collaboration between researchers and participatory budgeting sponsors. The implicit question raised in this project involves

D. Williams and D. Waisanen, *Real Money, Real Power?*,
https://doi.org/10.1007/978-3-030-59201-1_4

observation of the councilmember-sponsor in a natural setting. We hence wanted to limit collaboration as much as possible due to its potential to undermine observations. Our reports about transparency reflect the research experience under these circumstances.

Critical to this experience, PBNYC develops over multiple phases. The timing and exact form of implementation may vary by council district and by year. In general, the first phase is idea generation, which has multiple parts. In the 2018–2019 Cycle 8 in preparation for the FY 2020 budget, these parts included: (1) Sidewalk tables where members of the public could complete idea cards and, more generally, frequently circulated idea cards to be returned to council member offices; (2) websites located at http://ideas.pbnyc.org/ (in general for all participating council districts, with a mirror at https://shareabouts-pbnyc-2018.herokuapp.com/) and https://pbnyc39.com/idea-collection/ (controlled by Council Member Brad Lander's office); (3) idea-generating neighborhood assemblies open to the general public; (4) ideas brought by budget delegates in the second phase; (5) ideas generated in the budget delegate process; and (6) ideas otherwise communicated to the council member's office.

The second phase involves budget delegates who attend a delegate training session, meet with representatives of some city agencies, and then meet as delegates to formulate ballots. The PBNYC rule book describes this process as overseen by a district committee. The third phase involves promotional activities to advocate for projects on the ballot. Promotional activities could include various forms of communication, such as email from community groups that succeed in getting their projects onto the ballot, project expos (fairs where project advocates promote their projects), and advocacy at the time of balloting. The fourth phase involves voting, which occurs in two modes: (1) online and (2) at pop-up voting tables. For the 2018–2019 cycle, pop-up voting tables were scheduled between March 30 and April 7. The last phase involved the release of results and a related, celebratory event.

While these phases appear orderly and complete, the actual implementation is not. We observed that various council members omitted some elements such as neighborhood assemblies or project expos. In general, expos were conducted on the first day of voting at voting locations (which included schools that could have had projects on the ballot), while some districts may have omitted the expo altogether. Another researcher with whom the first author discussed this project at a conference suggested that some council member staff perform the budget delegate role. Also, one council member's office that we followed through the PB process appeared to combine some budget delegate training meetings with the meeting with city agency representatives. More important, there was no central method of learning of planned meetings or events by a central organization, leading to some missed opportunities. If there had been a central coordinator who shared information, we would have been able to construct our research plan earlier, attend more neighborhood assemblies and possibly find delegate meetings once we learned that one council member refused access. At the end of the day, the decentralized nature of PBNYC presents a monumental challenge to organizing equitable participation and deliberation, often confusing more than enlightening. We'll explore this finding in more detail.

In this light, our research plan aimed for qualitative observation at all PB phases, including post-decision focus groups for, at a minimum, two council districts. We hired two research assistants to attend neighborhood assembly and delegate meetings, and to collect data during other phases of the development process.[1] The only strict criterion for selecting the observed districts was districts with council members who had been involved in at least one prior participatory budgeting cycle. We intended to follow two selected council districts, but in one case this proved unworkable.

In the initial course of this research, difficulties arose almost immediately, providing a glimpse of what would become the running theme at the heart of this book's argument. As mentioned, contact with the city council staff determined that there is no central point for information about PB or PB processes. The staff at the city council did not (during our data collection process) have a centralized source of information (and this appears to have continued into the next cycle). The dates and locations of neighborhood assemblies could only be learned from individual council members' offices. Telephone calls to all 51 city council offices on, or before, September 17, 2018, determined that 33 council members were intending to engage in participatory budgeting.[2] However, only 17 provided dates of scheduled neighborhood assemblies! Others either had

[1] Graduate assistants were hired during September 2018 after receiving final grant approval from the Samuels Center and were engaged in observation after receiving IRB human subjects approval.

[2] PBNYC communication says there were 32 engaged districts in this cycle. Nevertheless, we had 33 positive responses.

not scheduled meetings, did not have the information readily available at their offices, or did not intend to have neighborhood assembly meetings.

One neighborhood assembly had already occurred and a few more were over before it was logistically possible to attend. After additional efforts, prospective dates were determined for 21 council districts, concurrent to the contact date determined for one council district,[3] and one district reported a date for an "info session" (not reported to be an idea-generating session). Of the 10 remaining, at least two had no assemblies, while others did not provide information.

Event observations were generally recorded in two forms. First, every observer made the same or nearly concurrent notes of the events. Second, most events were audio recorded.[4]

Meeting Variations

There is no singular participatory budgeting project in New York City. Instead, there are numerous participatory budget projects, as many as there are council members who engage in the practice. In Phase 1 of our observations, of importance to the citizen experience of participatory budgeting, there was almost no uniformity in the scheduling of these meetings. For the 22 council offices that provided information on neighborhood assemblies, the dates provided ranged from one to five, with a median of three.[5] Initial dates ranged from 9/17 to 10/2; and final dates ranged from 9/20 to 10/17. Only three sessions were on a weekend. Two of the weekend sessions and one weekday session were mid-day, while all the others were all in the evening starting between 5:30 p.m. and 7:00 p.m., often on the same day for many districts. One council

[3] I.e., logistically, if we learn of an event on the day it is happening, we cannot actually make use of the information. One of the events we learned about was on the same day we learned about it.

[4] No recording device was available for the first event. Additionally, one research assistant had technical difficulties with recordings for delegate meetings and interviews (discussed later) that led to an inability to transcribe the audio and meetings involving large numbers of people engaged in simultaneous small group activity that created too much noise (crosstalk) to produce usable transcripts, so our data collection strategies shifted over the course of research.

[5] Names mentioned in meetings and interviews, including public meetings, have been redacted. However, names mentioned in news media and names of (or other means of identifying) council members, are not.

member scheduled five sequential weekday evenings, while a different council member had three meetings spread over a month.

These findings beg the question of why so much variation occurred between districts? Shouldn't a process meant to be as inclusive as possible be administered in a standard way, so that everyone has an equal opportunity to participate and be part of the decision-making? At the very least, one of the most remarkable initial findings as we set out to do this research covering the processes for PBNYC was that citizen experience with something as simple as scheduling could itself be incredibly disorienting.

Based on this information, the first author and two research assistants individually, or sometimes together, attended seven neighborhood assemblies in Manhattan (three assemblies in three council districts), Brooklyn (one assembly/council district), and Queens (three assemblies in one council district). An assembly was staffed by one or more council staff, one or more experienced community members (in those districts with prior year PB) and, in many instances, a PB fellow sponsored by the Coro New York Leadership Center. Council members attended and spoke at some of these events.

The assembly involved two activities. The first activity provided an overview of the participatory budgeting process and an explanation of the difference between capital budget items (eligible in all districts) and expense items (generally ineligible). In 2016, planning for FY 2018, Council Member Brad Lander began allowing $50,000 of his expense discretionary funding to be decided through the PB process, explaining that he had noticed that many good ideas brought up in earlier years were disallowed because they did not meet the criteria for capital funding (Venugopal, 2016). In 2018 (planning for FY 2020), Council Member Stephen Levin also began to accept expense project proposals (Hanrahan, 2019).[6]

[6] In the broader budget process, the capital budget is funded by debt and the expense budget is funded through current revenue. These two budgets follow separate approval and expenditure processes. In the expense budget, funds must be specifically committed during the fiscal year and (typically) must be expended no later than a fiscal quarter after the end of the fiscal year (basically, enough time for an item to be delivered during the fiscal year, a bill received soon afterwards, and the payment to be processed). Except for the United States federal government, this is a universal practice, although the length of grace for bill processing differs by locality. Funds not expended by the end of the fiscal year (and grace period) revert (the authorization to expend them expires) to whatever fund

At the same time, some elements were reasonably consistent across most of the seven neighborhood assemblies. There was a discussion of the PB calendar: mentioning idea generation including the neighborhood assemblies and, in most instances, a mention of an online website for posting ideas; discussion of delegate meetings and, in some instances, invitations to become delegates; and a description of the project expos followed by voting, which could be online or at a voting location.[7] Some assemblies had a slide show that included topics such as empowerment, transparency, inclusion, equity, and community (see Fig. 4.1).

they came from to be committed again. Because of a funky New York State law resulting from the 1970s fiscal crisis, reverted money in the General Fund is hard to spend, but the city has a practice of transferring these funds to other funds where they can still be spent. In the capital budget, a multi-year capital plan is made. The first year of the capital plan is the budget for the upcoming fiscal year. The approved projects are committed during this year, but may take many years to complete. Capital fund authorization typically does not expire until the capital project is completed, although we think the city may deliberately expire some underfunded projects (project for which the authorized amount is deemed insufficient). Otherwise the funds remain available until the project is completed. All of that was necessary to explain that the council treats expense and capital funding as two independent practices. Council members are allocated two separate sums of money for capital and expense discretionary funding. The general amount of the capital discretionary funding has been fixed at $5 million for years. The speaker has more money, the exact amount of which is never clarified to our knowledge. The base expense allocation is much smaller ($500,000 plus $260,000 constrained to two categories $110,000 to aging, $150,000 to youth). It is generally allocated in small sums to each project (averaging $5000–$30,000 depending on council member preferences). Because expense funds go to immediate spending, the allocation is more visible and provides a more immediate benefit to the recipient. At the beginning of PB, council members chose to only allocate capital funds. We were not informed of their reasoning, but they frequently and prominently refer to $1 million, which would not be a realistic amount for their expense allocation. It is also possible that they want more control over the ability to produce immediate visible impacts, even if small. In 2016 (planning for FY 2018), one council member chose to expand his many year practice of capital-only PB to allow a small amount for expense budget PB. The next year, a second council member followed on.

[7]Some readers may find an explanatory element for each step helpful: The council member's staff brought up the future elements of the PB calendar. They would sometimes mention future neighborhood assemblies. At most assemblies they provided information directing attendees to a website where additional proposals could be submitted. The officials described the role of budget delegates as the people who meet to more fully develop projects and prepare the ballot and, most often, the invite attendees to consider becoming a delegate. They describe the overall process as extending over the fall and winter into the spring, during which there will be an opportunity to vote for the projects. Some assemblies had a slide show or video that describes participatory budgeting. Some of the slides displayed are shown in Fig. 4.1.

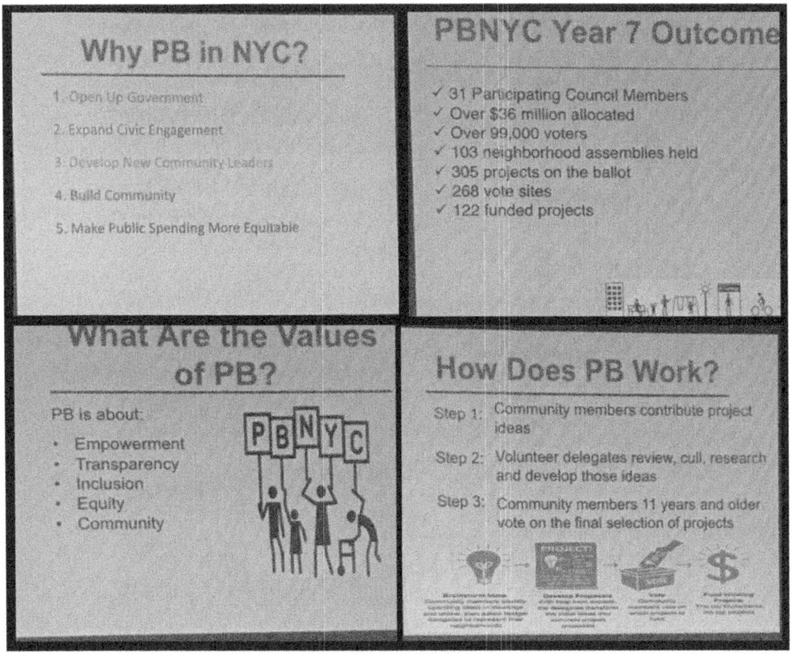

Fig. 4.1 Slides from a participatory budgeting meeting (*Source* Photograph by author)

Other slides included, for example, the prior year's results.

In the second activity, small groups meet, typically around tables, where the attendees propose ideas. Each small group is led by a facilitator, generally a community member who has been involved in prior years. Numerous ideas were proposed and added to oversize (roughly 25" × 35") paper posted near the tables, as shown in Fig. 4.2. But the tables were allowed to bring only a small fixed number (in some instances three) to a joint session at the end. At this joint session, a meeting facilitator (this role shifted several times over the course of this neighborhood assembly) called on a spokesperson from each group who presented their three selected projects to everyone present. While not overtly expressed, it was the observer's understanding that these projects would be carried forward to the delegate stage. As shown in Fig. 4.2, the selection was made through the use of stickers and hash marks.

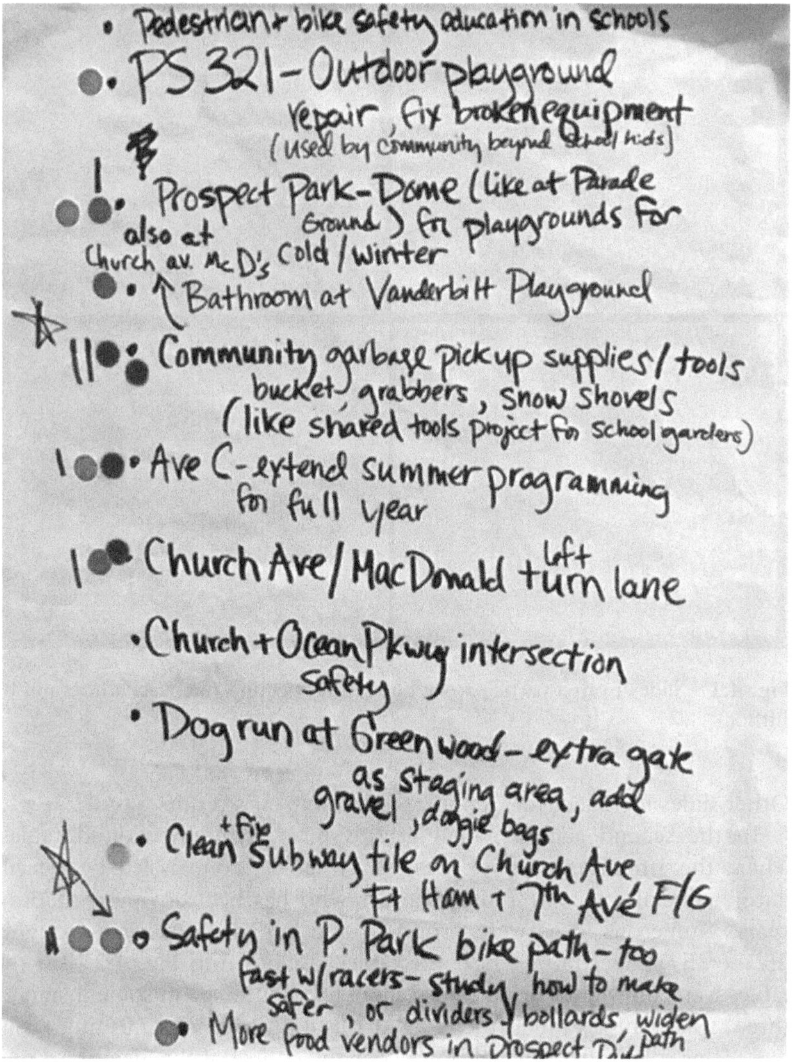

Fig. 4.2 Ideas generated (*Source* Photograph by author)

The observers were able to attend only one of these small groups during each of the neighborhood assemblies. Two of the events differed from this design. In one, only a handful of people attended, so the entire process was with the whole group and only a few ideas were generated. At another meeting, it became apparent that the neighborhood assembly was a precursor to a meeting for another purpose. Many people were at least somewhat confused about the meeting, as they had arrived for the other purpose: a discussion of a city project that was causing disruption in the neighborhood. Rather than having small group meetings, the representatives of the council office handed out idea suggestion cards. There was no final summarizing activity at this neighborhood assembly.

Top-Down Involvement

To gain a deeper sense of the multiple obstacles citizens might encounter, relative to issues such as potential clientelism, expert-driven decision-making, and more, observations at a variety of meetings in Phase 1 also presented some jarring findings relative to the larger entities citizens had to deal with in their deliberations. As we discussed in the introduction, the first neighborhood assembly we observed (in Manhattan) was held in a community center. Although a poster about participatory budgeting was visible from the street, the actual entrance was difficult to find. This meeting was brief and sparsely attended. Of the five neighborhood attendees observed, two were especially interested in becoming budget delegates. One of these two identified himself as a teacher.

At all three of the Queens neighborhood assemblies, the meetings were thematic, although at the last one there was permission to also propose any other capital project. The council office scheduled the meetings with themes attached, *thus predetermining the scope of projects*. The themes were schools, parks, and libraries. At the schools meeting most, if not all, attendees other than council staff and the observer were school employees. The attendees proposed projects focused on their own schools even though there were many other schools in the council district.[8] Experts appeared both as participants and as agency representatives in the vetting and costing process. The Queens neighborhood assemblies were focused on particular categories and attendees at each included, or

[8]With 1700 total public schools in New York, there are an average of 33 per council district.

in the case of schools, were dominated by experts from that domain. At both of the other meetings, there were a mixture of employees with interests related to the theme, and other individuals. Right from the get-go, we were left with the clear impression that many such meetings involved the usual suspects—those who had clear stakes in the theme (and rightly so), but in the absence of broader citizen topic selection and input, we couldn't help but feel that there was a type of "gamed" aspect to what was happening.

While you'd never find these types of messages in any official communication about PB, a surprising expectation for quid pro quo sometimes emerged in these seemingly deliberative forums. At the parks-themed neighborhood assembly, a facilitator, who is also a parks employee, said that "You need to make deals with other people to support each other's ideas."[9] This isn't to forgo the relationship building that is at the heart of getting work done in politics, but it did raise a question for us about what norms for idea generation, inclusion, and other opinions might be operating beyond such clear interest group-related remarks—threads we followed throughout the remainder of our research.

Many comments reflected the role of experts and top-down agency involvement in the meetings as well. At the parks-themed meeting, a fair amount of the discussion focused on trees and tree guards. An observer note refers to an expert who "is a tree researcher at [a well-known university] and has some very convincing stats that tree guards significantly increase the longevity of urban trees." Notes from that meeting show that tree guards were included in the projects referred from the neighborhood assembly to the delegate process. These data show the moderate influence of experts-as-participants in some districts. More important, though, at the parks-themed event, there are several comments reflecting decision shaping by the Park's Department:

Speaker 2: Is there any way to know what projects are in the [existing plan]....

Speaker 3: Parks has all the documents. They have a whole list on their website....

Speaker 2: Yeah, I wish they had that here for us right now....

[9] This quote is from observer notes, as it occurred during a noisy portion of the meeting.

The observations reviewed included many references to the influence of agency representatives. These included substantial concern over the lack of access to information. The positioning of needed resources with the Park's Department was only the beginning of what turned out to be a larger deference to the agency during the deliberations. In the following remarks, notice the anticipation with which speakers expected the department itself to involve itself in PB input. While passive influence is concerning, more concerning is the unexplained exercise of agency discretion[10]:

Speaker 4: if you want a water fountain in your park and there isn't one, the Parks Department is not going to see it that way….

Speaker 1: So that's what we have to find out. You're going to fight Parks…. Even when we go through this whole thing, they're going to say, "No, no, no, no."[11]

We were left with the impression that, even amid the small budget allocations that PB projects sum to, larger entities were expected to have a say and stake in what should matter to citizens. Amid these conversations, real money and real power seemed to come with limitations and qualifications.

In one part of the conversation, the costs attributed to enacting citizen budgeting allocations—whether perceived or real—were expected to be subject to top-down, exclusive judgments as well.

Speaker 1: I would think it wouldn't fit with our budget constraints, yeah.

Speaker 3: Just for one department issued [crosstalk].

Speaker 1: Everything requires so much money. It's like they think [it's the] Taj Mahal.

[10] Agency discretion can be correctly exercised because proposed projects may be genuinely beyond agency capacity or, as the capital budget is funded through municipal bonds which are federally regulated, they may be ineligible for such funding. The concern is that the comments noted do not reflect awareness of these sorts of explanations.

[11] All emphases (italics) in transcripts have been added.

Speaker 3: Because at one point, we're like, "We'll help pay for it," and they were like, "It's going to be $300 thousand dollars." "Well, we don't have the money."

Speaker 1 It's ridiculous.

So PB meetings are not as simple as generating and choosing among options (and, as mentioned, sometimes options are limited from the outset). Cost attributions figure into this picture as well, and citizens do not get to decide what kind of costs comparisons could be made when one agency that already has a lot of power of these matters gets to decide pricing. One participant noted how "if one of the Parks [representatives] could tell us what's in the pipeline, what's being done already, so we could have an idea … that might be helpful." Each step of the way, we found that the problem for citizen experience was not so much that there were park-related matters to deliberate over, but that the continuous invocation and deferral to parks' experts and representatives was needed to even have the conversation. In a way, the park acted as a kind of phantom interest group.

In fact, so much of this meeting was about what the parks department might or might not think about a change that speakers struggled to find an appropriate reach for a project that would neither be perceived as too small nor too big. Note in the following passage how the conversation begins and ends with the Parks Department's potential responses:

Speaker 4: I don't want to knock out your [named] Park, but we're going to put it up to vote on the thing, but I've been hearing everybody, from you, and from Speaker 5, that it seems like it was dead a few times over already. [crosstalk]. We're talking about doing the thing before [crosstalk] are they refusing [to fix it]?

Speaker 3: Not refusing to fix it. That they're not responsible to fix it, I think. I think you have to go to the Council people. So, that's why I was here.

Speaker 1: Yeah, with Parks, they're going to refuse everything anyway. Put everything down [crosstalk].

Speaker 4: I misheard. I thought he was saying that he was aware of it, because you guys were talking, and it seemed like it wasn't happening in the Parks end. That's why I said they serve underserved neighborhoods. They're focusing on that. They're doing a lot, so they might not want to look at that right now. But I thought that he was specifically told that. That's cool, if you weren't.

Speaker 1: But one of the jobs, they're not really interested in doing it. For whatever reason, maybe too small, maybe they don't bother. Parks put the kibosh on everything.

This isn't to obviate the very real difficulties of costs and implementation—and the Parks Department's role in fostering or hindering (or acting as a check and balance) against the citizen deliberation. But what's interesting is the spirit of chronic opposition testified to in each speaker's remarks. If there is real money and real power at play, it is far from unlimited.

Compared to the Queens meetings, the Brooklyn neighborhood assembly reflected a very different tenor. We found ourselves asking why. It had a sophisticated organization with numerous well-organized volunteer leaders and direct links to an external nonprofit organization (the NYC-based Participatory Budgeting Project). While almost all meetings had an overview session followed by an idea-generating session, in council district 39 (Brooklyn), it had a more professional flavor. The examples drawn and discussed in Figs. 1 and 2 are from this meeting and demonstrate some of the procedures used.

The obstacles we observed continued across jurisdictions, most notably due to the ad hoc, hastily assembled feel of many of the meetings. The second Manhattan neighborhood assembly appeared to be inserted, possibly opportunistically, before another meeting on a different topic. There was no public signage indicating that a PB meeting was occurring. Many attendees appeared confused about what was happening (one of the researchers recollects that people were saying things like "What's this about?" and "Where is the meeting about the L train?"). The meeting was held in a location where people were required to show an ID to enter—an additional barrier. However, as it progressed an alternate door was opened allowing attendance without an ID.

Some organization did exist for citizen input. An observer note indicates one member of the public asked for planning material so that ideas could be coordinated with what the city is already doing. At several meetings, "Idea Cards" (see Fig. 4.3) were distributed to attendees. This was the only form of idea generation and gathering at the second Manhattan neighborhood assembly.[12]

[12] The card is also available in Spanish on the reverse.

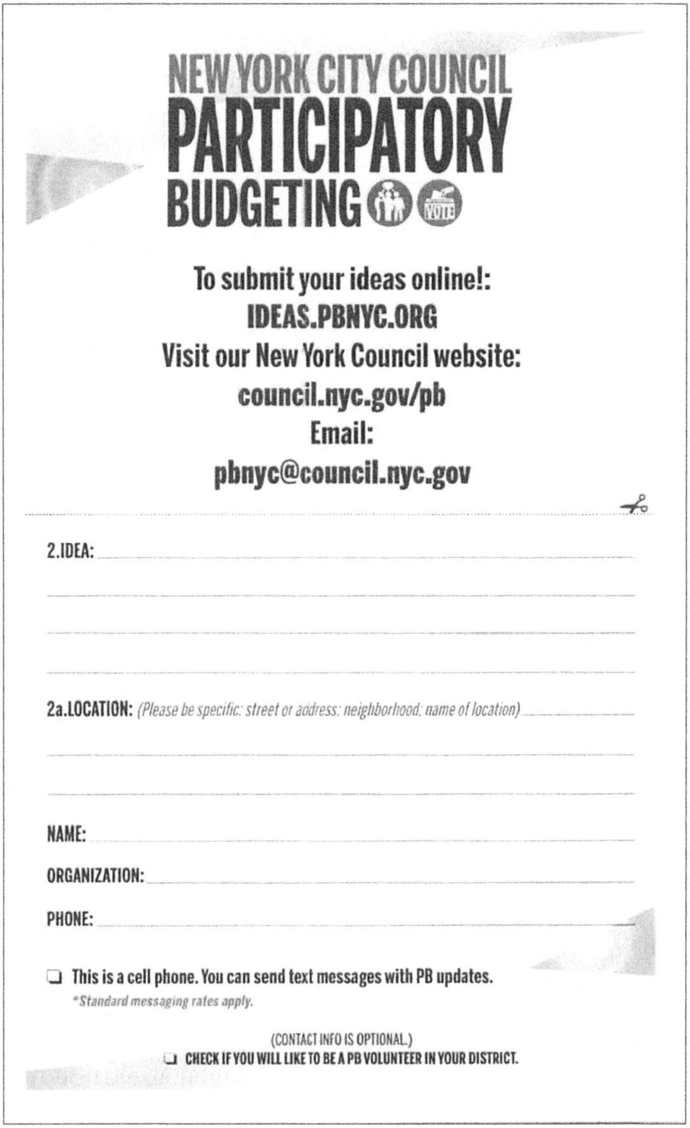

NEW YORK CITY COUNCIL
PARTICIPATORY
BUDGETING

To submit your ideas online!:
IDEAS.PBNYC.ORG
Visit our New York Council website:
council.nyc.gov/pb
Email:
pbnyc@council.nyc.gov

2.IDEA: ______

2a.LOCATION: *(Please be specific: street or address: neighborhood: name of location)* ______

NAME: ______

ORGANIZATION: ______

PHONE: ______

❑ This is a cell phone. You can send text messages with PB updates.
Standard messaging rates apply.

(CONTACT INFO IS OPTIONAL.)
❑ CHECK IF YOU WILL LIKE TO BE A PB VOLUNTEER IN YOUR DISTRICT.

Fig. 4.3 Idea card (*Source* Distributed at neighborhood assemblies)

At several meetings, attendees were also encouraged to review a map of the council district to determine whether they were potential participants and, perhaps, for them to consider where projects might be considered.

In these meetings, again the top-down involvement—and the exclusivity of this involvement—returned as a theme. Particularly around matters of cost setting, the procedures that are laid out for citizens are subject to the influence of usually one centralized authority. At the third Manhattan neighborhood assembly we heard the following exchange:

Speaker 6: And is that ... are these amounts that get approved based on like a bid or?

Speaker 2: So, what would happen is, you would come up with sort of the general idea in the budget delegate meetings and work on all that and then we would send them to the various city agencies. So, say it's something resurfacing ... actually, no, let's go with ... yeah, like resurfacing the NYCHA sidewalk repair. We would come up with idea and then we would send that idea over to the DOT. We would send it over to DOT. DOT would look over that idea and come back to us with a price estimate for that. So, that's how we get the price estimates.

Although the citizen deliberation is expected to be replete with proliferating ideas and expanded choices, when it comes to the actual numbers allocated for particular projects, ironically, there's little choice. Without any competitive bidding, the room for someone at an agency to set a participatory budgeting agenda by deeming one project too small and insignificant a cost to undertake, or too large and expensive, is actually quite large here. Even more important is the sense from those at these meetings that this isn't minimal oversight—top-down entities are expected to exert a great deal of influence over the PB stages.

From each of the seven meetings attended, we noted that the following ideas that were approved at the neighborhood assemblies in Table 4.1. Manhattan 1 was sparsely attended, only one idea is shown in observer notes. Manhattan 2 did not include a summary session and focused on idea cards, the contents of which were not shared, so we excluded that meeting from our analysis.

Table 4.1 Ideas approved at neighborhood assemblies

Manhattan 1	*Manhattan 3*	*Brooklyn*
Renovate school playground	Playground renovation School entry renovation Garden space/greenhouse Convert empty lot Camera security for park Increase public building accessibility	Traffic redesign Cleanup supply "share closet" Park bike path safety issue iPads for 5th grades Renovate school bathrooms Traffic calming Stop sign Outdoor seating at library High speed internet
Queens 1 (Schools)	*Queens 2 (Parks)*	*Queens 3 (Libraries and open call)*
Tech upgrade (2 schools mentioned) Gym equipment Hydroponic garden/science lab Auditorium upgrade	Workout equipment at a park Basketball court at a park 50 tree guards Enhance a park with dog park (2 parks mentioned) Enhance a park with skate park Phone charger fixtures at a park General renovation of a park (2 parks mentioned) Enhance a park with greenspace	Upgrade a public library (2 libraries mentioned) Improve a school library Add a second floor to a library Add a rooftop garden to a library New stage equipment at a school Greenspace at a playground Countdown clocks at a bus stop Auditorium upgrade at a school

Source Observer notes

In the next chapter, we look at the challenges of the next stage of the PB process. By seeking to gain access to and embed ourselves in many of these events, we gained a number of insights focusing on the ideals versus the reality of PB.

References

Venugopal, N. (2016, March 25, 28). Here's how you can vote for Brooklyn School Diversity or Book-Drop Boxes. *DNA Info: Cobble Hill, Carroll Gardens & Red Hook* (Online).

Hanrahan, L. (2019, March 25). Cast your ballot in the district 33 participatory budgeting vote next week. *Greenpoint Post*. Retrieved from https://greenpointpost.com/cast-your-ballot-in-the-district-33-participatory-budgeting-vote-next-week.

CHAPTER 5

The Challenges of Delegate Meetings

Abstract This chapter reviews experiences observing budget delegate training meetings and one delegate meeting. It reviews a denial of access to other meetings and some alternative data collection that reveals that budget delegate meetings occur behind closed doors. This opacity is particularly concerning because of evidence that many delegates are present as advocates of particular projects and participants are over-represented by relatively well-off members of the community, while many disadvantaged participants lack adequate resources to be delegates. We discuss issues of equity, inclusion, the lack of transparency, and issues involving project advocacy through an exploration of media content connected to these meetings.

Keywords Delegate · Disadvantaged · Equity · Inclusion · Media

In this chapter, we unpack the central themes at issue in Phase 2 of our observations at the delegate meetings. Each research assistant attended one delegate training session. At that point the research was paused because one of the council offices notified the PI that delegate meetings are closed to the public.[1] We were stunned. Why would a process

[1] As a result, the human subjects application had to be revised before further action could be taken.

D. Williams and D. Waisanen, *Real Money, Real Power?*,
https://doi.org/10.1007/978-3-030-59201-1_5

grounded in the ideals of public participation be closed at any juncture? What content would be discussed or procedures would be used that would make any stakeholder want to prevent others from having access to the meeting?

Much of the delegate process, where the most important agenda setting decisions are made, was closed to the research process. Pozen (2019) argues that transparency is not a good in itself, rather it is an instrumental good for the purpose of assuring good governance and good public service. Thus, the expectation of transparency in a particular setting requires nuance and justification. For the PBNYC, there are two particular reasons why transparency should be expected. First, an underlying theme of PB as presented by representatives of the PB entities, emphasizes transparency as a purpose of PB. It is not unreasonable to expect the PBNYC process to exhibit a value that is itself promoted by PBNYC. Second, an asserted objective of PBNYC is to share power. Obscuring the decision process by hiding the agenda setting component is contrary to this objective.

Given the thicket of issues at stake, we pursued questions around this topic as far as possible. When the research was restarted with added notification, the council office still rejected access to its delegate meetings. The other council office did not overtly refuse access; however, it provided meeting dates and times only after our repeated efforts. As a result, only one delegate meeting was attended. Because of timing and logistics, no other council office was reached for observation of additional delegate meetings before the timeframe of the delegate meetings expired. When we started this research, we did not expect access to be a problem, but it became a guiding indictment in tracking the citizen experience of PB.

Equity and Inclusion

Looking away from the ideals of PBNYC to the actual experience of what it's like to be a citizen in these processes, the delegate sessions revealed a key issue: who was at these meetings and who they served. That participants had some attentiveness to this topic provides room for hope. Yet the inadequacies of PB to currently address them loomed large given how many of the "already served" and "overserved" participate in these sessions.

The first delegate training meeting was comprised of two main phases. The first phase (after a brief introduction) combined a slideshow presentation with substantial discussion. The second phase involved a question and answer session. The first slides discussed the process for the meeting. The council office predetermined the delegate categories as education; culture and community facilities; parks and environment; and youth. There was substantial discussion of "whittling" the hundreds of proposals to a small number for the ballot. Two principles are discussed, financial conflict of interest (you can propose, but not vote) and equity and inclusion, a topic that repeats several times through the conversation and leads to substantial discussion. In the following remarks, the issue of who is served comes to the fore:

Speaker 5: To the question earlier about neighborhoods that are underserved and how do we ensure that they're represented, I just kind of want to do a little poll quiz kind of in the room. So, who is from [i.e. Neighborhood 1: the wealthiest neighborhood in the district]?[2] If you could raise your hand. Who's from, I don't know [inaudible: Neighborhood 2]? Again, these are the people that will be looking at the ideas and then narrowing them down to the projects in which the entire community votes on, so just be very mindful of the folks that are stewarding the process along. Who is from [Neighborhood 3]? That's awesome. We definitely need those ideas. [Neighborhood 4]? What do we got? [crosstalk: Neighborhood 5].

Speaker 7: [Neighborhood 6]. [crosstalk].

Speaker 5: Okay. So just wanted everyone to notice that at least half of the room is from [Neighborhood 1] and [I] just wanted to name that and pay attention to that.

Although delegates are admonished to exhibit concern for the underserved, they are likely to be relatively well-off members of the community. Likely because the topics of equity and inclusion are raised as ideals in these meetings, at least the speaker keeps the group focused on what

[2] Neighborhood wealth determined by income map at https://project.wnyc.org/median-income-nation/

participation means in the context of participatory budgeting. The fissures between what should and does happen started to present themselves in the very idea that citizens have to show up for PB sessions.

Speaker 7: But we're not going out to underserved neighborhoods to highlight their problems. People need to come to the committee with their ideas.

Speaker 2: Well, yes and no. I'll give you an example for my first year. We were [inaudible] on the education committee and we got a bunch of ideas from the neighborhood assemblies and one delegate halfway through said how many schools are there in the district? 17. They were like there's only eight schools here. They're like can we go out and go and ask these other schools? We were already halfway through the process and people were like wait a minute. These people already have ideas. It's not fair to them. We're like that's the point of PB. Ultimately, the group decided, and we asked [inaudible] can we do this because nobody knew the rules. We're like, "Yeah. You guys figure it out." So, everybody chose a different school, contacted the principal and we actually got a few visional ideas that would have not happened. So, you're not limited by the ideas that are submitted at the time that you start this process.

Speaker 7: Exactly, because we're talking about underserved neighborhoods and the neighborhoods represented here are pretty well served.

Speaker 2: Yes.

Speaker 7: Because we're the people who are paying attention and are able to attend meetings and able to volunteer.

At the heart of this discussion, the speakers tussle with issues of representation, how the usual suspects tend to show up to PB meetings, and most importantly, who exactly has the time, attention, and resources to volunteer for democracy. Speaker 2 lays out that, practically speaking (and there is some room for optimism in these remarks), in the first year the education committee just decided to reach out to the schools themselves rather than waiting for those representing these institutions across the area to show up to a session. It takes citizens to pull out a key fact for what's happening: PB's very structure and stages may prevent the sessions from being as inclusive as they might. That the participant worked with the principals in the district is also telling. This was surely an effort to be inclusive, but going to the heads of these institutions rather than other community stakeholders (teachers, students, staff) evidenced another way that equity and inclusion are so easily bypassed.

Despite the presence of the already served or overserved, what we did learn is that one person can make a substantial difference in forcing these considerations. Speaker 1 eloquently argued that:

> This is, I think, one of the things you're going to grapple with and I think it's one of the great questions about democracy. What it means [inaudible] inequality, how much of the goal is to attend to and serve underserved or disenfranchised communities or places that have been left out and how much of the goal is to provide good, strong, public institutions because if we don't have them in all neighborhoods ... You could argue that [Neighborhood 1] doesn't need a library because people can just afford to go to the bookstore. But democracy does setup libraries in all our neighborhoods, the richer and the poor. So, this is what's on you is to try to figure out how to balance this out. ... You can scan the ideas from what's there already to try to help you but this is how it works. Those questions are on us and on the ballot. They're on you.

The context for these comments can be found in the words of George Washington Plunkitt: "If there's a fire in Ninth, Tenth, or Eleventh Avenue, for example, any hour of the day or night, I'm usually there with some of my election district captains as soon as the fire engines. If a family is burned out I don't ask whether they are Republicans or Democrats, and I don't refer them to the Charity Organization Society, which would investigate their case in a month or two and decide they were worthy of help about the time they are dead from starvation. I just get quarters for them, buy clothes for them if their clothes were burned up, and fix them up till they get things runnin' again. It's philanthropy, but it's politics, too — mighty good politics. Who can tell how many votes one of these fires bring me" (Plunkitt & Riordon, 1905, pp. 51–52)? These words occur in the chapter "To Hold Your District, Study Human Nature and Act Accordin'," where he makes clear that his largess, or at least his empathy, is spread around to all, whatever their station in life.[3] Similarly, the very existence of PB at least makes the presence or absence of what's available to one's community—and surrounding communities—an issue for public discussion. Even if the structure or processes available might be imperfect, having a forum communicating that democratic budget allocations should be within more people's reach might grow their own legs, so to speak.

Another speaker demonstrated this point, building off of the last speaker's remarks:

Speaker 5: Yeah. Before we kind of move on, just to kind of relate to some of that. ... I went through the census tracks for everyone in the district and a lot of the places ... There's a lot of $30,000 or $40,000 households like average median household income, $30,000–$40,000 especially in the southern part of the district. So, if you look at [the council district] as a whole I think it's like 80, 90. It's a good amount. It's definitely upper middle class, but I knew that that wasn't the whole story. So, I kind of dug in a little bit and the census tracks are only going to 1000–1500 people. In many parts of the district there are many $20,000–$30,000 average median household incomes. So, it really is incumbent on us to be noticing that and to lift them up as much as possible.

[later returning to the topic]

Speaker 11: One other thing about parks is a lot of ideas come in about [a large park]. So, we talked about the needs analysis. We had that tension where on the one hand the delegates had this obligation to look for other places that

[3] Plunkitt's point is that political success is achieved by delivering benefits to the public. He accomplished this through a combination of "honest graft" and the use of a portion of that graft to meet the needs of his district. He does not provide for public programs that anticipate those needs and have resources on hand; in fact, he disparages that approach. He wants the public to know that it is he, George Washington Plunkitt, who made sure those needs were met. Removing the graft and replacing it with earmarks, a similar process is described in the comments above. The resources are not made available in the first place, they are withheld until there is an opportunity to provide them in a public way. The analogy is not exact, but the basic approach, public delivery of benefits for voters, remains.

> might benefit more from the parks [because the park] has the [a focused support group], but most of the ideas from [the park] and so many people from all over the city use [the park] that is just not for the people in the neighborhood.

In both speakers' comments, the plot thickens. Both are guided by a responsibility to make the budget process and eventual allocations as equitable and inclusive as possible, yet an overriding disconnect between current and needed knowledge, and their positionalities in these forums versus the spaces and places where those could make a difference operate, permeates their talk.

Other topics at this delegate training meeting included repeated discussion of the need to reduce the hundreds of proposals to a small number. Many are eliminated by a determination that they are not viable, but viability varies from not eligible, to costing too much within the scope of the council member's commitment of discretionary funds, to possible exclusion for unspecified reasons by the city agencies (as argued in the last chapter, that gives top-down entities a great deal of power in these matters). However, after all of this trimming, this happened:

> *Speaker 5*: So [the Education Committee] is a double committee. So, the Arts and Culture Committee as well as the Education Committee, there will be six projects that go on to the public ballot that the community will vote on. So that seems pretty daunting. Like there's 100, 200 ideas. A lot of the ideas will be duplicative or not feasible for several reasons or they'll be as vague as "having fun" and they kind of just drop off. So, I think last year we only had 8 to 10 viable projects and from the 8 to 10 we chose six.

Although we observed an intention to provide consideration for (if not actual voice to) the underserved, of the most significance to this project, *no access was provided to observe this intention in practice*, since the council office refused our access to delegate meetings. Citizens clearly wrestled with equity and inclusion throughout this process, but those intentions may matter very little. The critical turning point is when/what ideas get reduced to those that will go up for public consideration—but the lack of transparency toward that step leaves open for the already served, the overserved, and a variety of top-down single agency or special/clientalistic interests to enter the picture and choose only those deemed important to a narrow group.

In fact, continuing the theme of top-down involvement from first PB stage, there were several remarks concerning city agencies that substitute their practices and preferences to those of the PB committees:

Speaker 5: So, I've had people that have an idea for an expense project or buying technology at this school and it's only going to cost $2000, which would be ineligible for an expense project. So, the idea in the bundling piece would be to get three schools and then buy $2000 worth of equipment for three schools and … then that would have put you into the eligibility category at least for the costing. That's not a guarantee or anything but just to kind of define what we mean by bundling.

Speaker 2: And the example there is that the Department of Sanitation doesn't allow you to … If you want to do a bunch of street trash cans they don't allow you to bundle them so that you can do two things. … One trash can itself is not enough to be a capital project so that agency specifically says you can't do that so that may come up.

The point here is that Department of Sanitation applies administrative rules that, at a minimum, are not explained to the PB participants. The Department of Sanitation has an administrative rule that prevents the bundling of smaller objects to make a capital project (the minimum cost in 2018 when this happened was $35,000). This administrative rule might be reasonable, although it appears inconsistent with a different administrative rule at the Department of Education that allows the bundling of computers to achieve a target value. Whether reasonable or not, the PB participants don't understand that it ultimately expresses an arbitrary view.

Wrestling with larger city agencies certainly brought into view how much equity and inclusion the participants in these meetings felt they had too, since so much of what was being discussed was accountable to agency or representative oversight. Sometimes the speakers wrestled with the crossings of these agencies—who has what jurisdiction with certain budgeting matters—for instance, as one participant asked the others if there was "in the past another committee for traffic and would that fall under parks and environment this year?" Another speaker replied that it may be a possibility, since the Department of Transportation "doesn't want to be a part of this process." Figuring out which agencies should be involved, for what reasons, and whether or not these desires were laid out in stone somewhere, or simply the preference of some individual or group within constituted barriers to the deliberative processes.

Research notes from the second delegate training meeting show several topics of interest.[4] First, delegates are seated in groups according to the category they will examine. Second, the notes do not describe an overview session, instead this session includes meeting with agency representatives. This fact leaves it unclear whether the council office held another prior meeting that was not communicated to the research team, or whether, instead, this council office simply combined the two types of meetings. Because of this arrangement, the observer joined one of the groups. A specific research note indicates an agency representative asked each person in that group, "what's your project idea?", which the observer understood to mean that the delegate was present to represent his or her own project—bringing further into view the challenge of equity and inclusion at this stage.

A desire for information that was not readily available or available in a form usable in council district-level decision-making also arose in the meeting between delegates and agencies. A back and forth between a delegate and an agency representative concerning projects that are already planned proves illustrative:

> The delegate asks, "Can we see the list of underway projects to figure out what is redundant?" The agency representative responds, "Your councilmember can provide that list."
>
> The delegate asks, "Could we have seen the list *before* the neighborhood assemblies?" The agency representative does not directly answer.
>
> The delegate asks, "How can we know what is a valid idea before seeing this list?' The agency representative does not provide a response.

[4] This session is not supported by a transcript.

Through this passive failure to assist with this information the participants are denied insight into what might be pointless requests because the projects are already planned; but they are also denied insight into the kinds of projects that might make sense. An observational note further indicates: "Next, committees will refine ideas, later submit formally to Parks who will weigh in again and provide estimates for individual project costs. These will be the numbers that appear on the ballot." In terms of equity and inclusion, the PB participants have inadequate access to information and the agency representative does not take steps to resolve it. Instead, participants are referred to a website that has so much information that the PB participants cannot process it (at one stage) and refer them to their council office at another. The decisions in this meeting are finalized except for costs, and it isn't clear how or when the cost information will be incorporated into the ballot.

In consultation with another primary researcher, we were provided a handout that the New York City Department of Transportation [DOT] distributed by an agency/delegate. The DOT handout says: "DOT urges PB Transportation Committees to nominate existing DOT capital projects for PB funding."[5] We were told that when DOT supplied the handout, they also said that they would oppose any other capital projects. These communications indicate that at least for some types of projects, agencies exhibit determined expert effort to shape the proposed projects. These efforts mirror the consultation process associated with community board agency consultations and suggest a future that will reflect capture by the agencies. With respect to the validating role that experts play, it is clear they exhibit considerable influence and the comments strongly suggest that this influence is not simply through the expert determination of project eligibility, but also, to an unknown degree, the substitution of organizational-based preferences in place of the organically arising community preferences.

The last meeting observed was a single delegate session.[6] This was apparently the last delegate meeting for this district. Among the participants were leaders from previously observed neighborhood assemblies and

[5] This shared information is included with permission from the original researcher.

[6] No transcript is available for this meeting. As mentioned in an earlier note, the GA had a set of audio files that were, in fact, blank. He did not know why they were blank. The answer given is "technical issues."

the delegate training session. The session involved groups by category. We noted:

> The format of this meeting is similar to the neighborhood assemblies to the extent that the groups are sitting around discussing and refining ideas – [the] main difference now is that there are rough quotes on cost of proposals.

The observer followed the school's related session. The final proposed projects, to be submitted for a final cost estimate, specifically target the schools from which teachers are attending the session.

Opacity and Advocacy

Because of the denied access, we modified the remainder of the observation agenda to include many publicly available and other data focused on the delegate meetings. First, documents were collected from the internet and from council members. There was a wide search for internet postings, including: (a) all identifiable news media postings, focusing on smaller local media, (b) all identifiable postings from the council offices, and (c) social media postings from council members and their offices. Council members were also asked for copies of newsletters for the period beginning early in 2018. Only a limited number were provided. Table 5.1 lists all of the items that we examined.

Our goal was to study the degree to which information about the budget delegate process is communicated to the public. In total, 1592

Table 5.1 PB Items Examined

Item	*Number*	*Item*	*Number*
News media	**1295**	**Council communications**	**297**
Blog post	101	Council.nyc	100
Online news papers	1164	Council member web pages	57
Online magazines	5	Newsletters	62
Online multimedia	25	Facebook feed	63
		Twitter feed	15
Total all forms			1592

items were collected as pdf files, which were either saved as searchable or converted to searchable documents with OCR software. Some Facebook and Twitter feeds were broken into segments, so the total number of sites visited is somewhat fewer. Items ranged in length from a half page or less to 318 pages (a Twitter feed).

The search was conducted using current online sources found through Google using "participatory budget" as the search term and limited to New York City, supplemented by further searching through identified online news media using the media's search options; and searching for and through the Twitter and Facebook sites of PB engaged council members. The search was focused primarily on the most recent year first, followed by a search back to the first year of New York City's participatory budgeting program in 2011. There are some duplicate items, as some publishers of online newspapers publish more than one newspaper and use identical, or nearly identical, articles with more than one newspaper. Although extensive, the search could not be exhaustive.

The 1592 items were searched for the term "delegate" to focus on this portion of the PB process, resulting in 240 items (see Table 5.2) for further review. Of these, eight were found to use the term "delegate" with other meanings—such as references to other sorts of delegates, or use of the term as a verb—leaving 232 that mention budget delegates. Of these, only one Facebook feed, which is mirrored with two links, provided one advance notice of a series of budget delegate meetings. In comparison, these items contain six advance notices of budget delegate

Table 5.2 Classification of Content

Notices and calendar Mention		*Substantial content*		*Limited or other content*	
Classification	*Count*	*Classification*	*Count*	*Classification*	*Count*
Meeting notice	1(2)[a]	Call for delegates	21	Brief mention	13
Training notice	6	Delegate narrative	30	On to next stage	30
Other notice	14	General description	95		
Calendar overview	27	Praise/Thank you	28	Other meanings	8
		Cost obstacle	2		
Total	48(49)	Total	176	Total	51

[a]There was only one prior notice of a delegate meeting, it appeared in two mirrored posts

Note This table sums to more than 240 because some items are tagged with more than one classification

training meetings (where no decisions take place), 14 advance notices of neighborhood assemblies and other sorts of events, and 27 overviews of the then-forthcoming participatory budgeting calendars, without specific dates. Other remarks about delegate meetings include one Twitter notice of a meeting that was concurrently taking place and Facebook pages that contain photos or comments referencing meetings that have taken place in the days just before the posts.

If there's any finding that emerged from these data, it's that many budget delegate meetings for PBNYC are opaque and filled with insurmountable barriers to many citizens. The budget delegate meetings, in which the most critical decisions are made, are not communicated to the public in advance of the meetings. We found no evidence that council offices provide systematic public notice or open access to budget delegate meetings. Furthermore, the texts that we searched testified to many of these themes and more. The following are some specific comments from news media of note.

Concerning the inability to be a delegate, we learned that "For some, however, the time investment was an unconquerable barrier. Gracie Xavier, a Flatbush resident, reflects that she was 'not as involved' as she should have been. But she also says that meetings conflicted with her work schedule" (Whitman, 2012, para. 10). Beyond what we found in attending meetings, there's a wealth of reactions along similar lines—PB processes do not make it easy to be a delegate. Concerning the way delegates are selected, Guarino (2015) establishes that "Starting this year, the councilman's office will be asking each civic association and other organizations to select a delegate. They will work with and train these delegates who will then solicit ideas from the community" (para. 14). Here in microcosm is the top-down and representation problem we had seen in both the first and second stages. Equity issues abound, for instance, with "Mott Haven resident Carmen Aquino [who] said she is worried so many of the budget delegates are from Manhattan. 'How is it going to be fair for us to propose projects? How many of those projects that we are going to propose are really going to get funding?'" (Robinson, 2011, para. 8–9).

Concerning access or delegate commitment, Rom (2016) notes how, "Citywide, in 2014 fewer than half of those who signed up to be delegates at the beginning of the process ended up serving actively through the delegate phase, even as the number of participants has grown yearly, according to a report put out by the Urban Justice Center" (para. 41). What starts with excitement about PB too often does not equal the necessary follow-through for what, to many, can be a very long process. Tied into these themes is a noteworthy discouragement about both the means and ends of PB: "'We have some projects that have been backed up for years,' said Dan Mundy Jr, president of the Broad Channel Civic Association. 'Some of my delegates won't come anymore because they feel that after all the effort they have put in nothing has come out of it'" (Gelfand, 2016, para. 3). What's clear is that for many citizens the time and effort have not matched the expectations heralded by PB for real money and real power.

Despite PB's opacity, we found evidence suggesting that delegates engage as delegates to promote specific projects. Delegates come to the meetings not necessarily to generate ideas or sift many notable options, but, in many instances, to engage as advocates. One report revealed that "Shields was a budget delegate last year, but his pet project, funding another soccer turf near the Fulton Houses on W. 17th St., wasn't selected" (Rack, 2015, para. 24). Another covered a teenager who "was one of the 'delegates' who backed one of the competing proposals during the months of preparation before the voting. He said he put in roughly 25 hours of work toward the cause, including attending meetings with Johnson's staff, as well as LAB School community members." Ultimately, "the proposal to get money for a new public address system for the school fell short. But a concerted effort to rally support through the P.T.A. and among students 'flushed out' the vote for the bathroom idea, though city funding will ultimately come through another channel" (Z. Williams, 2015a, para. 18).

We learned that "With tens of thousands of potential voters, delegates said they would focus on mobilizing their own supporters through community groups, canvassing and phone-banking rather than knocking competing projects" (Z. Williams, 2015b, para. 23). At the same time, "Muhlenberg Library Manager Lateshe Lee noted that her patrons would be 'really excited' about the win, 'because they've been asking us about it for the past couple of weeks.' The road to success was a long one — this was the second year the library appeared on the ballot, and it was through the work of outside delegates (along with some custom bookmarks getting out the word to vote) that finally secured a win" (Egan, 2016, para. 10). It is clear that delegates are advocates for particular projects; however, it is not clear whether they arrive as advocates or become advocates during the delegate process. News media reports are more ambiguous on this than some of the other forms of data collection with which we engaged. While delegates are shown to be advocates of projects, news media have no obligation to clarify this, and the lack of clarity suggests yet another reason why more transparency is needed.

Such unknowns contribute to the opacity of PB processes as played out on the ground. The experience of the delegate meetings, in general, is one with closed boundaries, discouragement, elite dominance, and people acting on behalf of particular interests rather than as deliberatively democratic citizens in pursuit of community-generated budget allocations. In the next chapter, we move to the next stage of observations: the project expos and pop-up voting procedures. It is in this stage that the problems of equity and inclusion and opacity and advocacy become especially clear.

References

Pozen, D. E. (2019). Seeing transparency more clearly. *Public Administration Review*. https://doi.org/10.1111/puar.13137.

Plunkitt, G. W., & Riordon, W. L. (1905). *Plunkitt of Tammany Hall: A series of very plain talks on very practical politics*. New York: McClure, Phillips & Co.

Whitman, E. (2012, April 16). Participatory budgeting hits New York City. *The Nation* (Online).

Guarino, D. (2015, October 9). Full plate at Rockaway Beach Civic. *The Wave*. Retrieved from https://www.rockawave.com/articles/full-plate-at-rockaway-beach-civic/.

Robinson, A. (2011, November 13). How to spend a million bucks. *Mott Haven Herald*. Retrieved from http://www.motthavenherald.com/2011/11/13/how-to-spend-a-million-bucks/.

Rom, G. (2016, January 29). Participatory budgeting hits a roadblock in Queens. *TimesLedger*. Retrieved from https://www.timesledger.com/stories/2016/5/pbarticle_2016_01_29_q.html.

Gelfand, A. (2016, November 25). Participatory budget community meeting. *The Wave*. Retrieved from https://www.rockawave.com/articles/participatory-budget-community-meeting/.

Rack, Y. (2015, October 15). Have your say—Participatory budgeting is back. *The Villager*. Retrieved from https://www.thevillager.com/2015/10/have-your-say-participatory-budgeting-is-back/.

Williams, Z. (2015a, May 14). Chelsea parks, Village library loo are big winners in participatory budgeting. *The Villager*. Retrieved from https://www.thevillager.com/2015/05/chelsea-parks-village-library-loo-are-big-winners-in-participatory-budgeting/.

Williams, Z. (2015b, April 2). Local projects want your vote! $1M up for grabs. *The Villager*. Retrieved from https://www.thevillager.com/2015/04/local-projects-want-your-vote-1m-up-for-grabs/.

Egan, S. (2016, May 19). Participatory budgeting funds new trees, cool Breezes. *The Villager*. Retrieved from https://www.thevillager.com/2016/05/participatory-budgeting-funds-new-trees-cool-breezes/.

CHAPTER 6

The Challenges of Project Expos and Pop-Up Voting

Abstract This chapter reviews observations and field interviews at project expos and pop-up voting locations. Some of the more significant findings were that all budget delegate interviewees who proposed projects were successful in getting their projects included on ballots, while only two of seven individuals who were not delegates found their projects on ballots. Most respondents had not engaged in participatory budgeting in earlier stages and three-fifths of these reported that they were unaware of participatory budgeting before they arrived at a public location for voting. Others reported family and work constraints, reflecting the same lack of resources we analyzed in Chapter 4. We identify issues of legitimacy, tokenism, and opportunities missed. We break down meeting attendance, suggested projects, prior year participation, and vote advocacy to determine who or what has influence at this stage of events. A particular concern were a few responses that expressed distrust over costs associated with projects.

Keywords Project expos · Pop-up voting · Legitimacy · Tokenism · Advocacy

In this third phase of our observations, we examined project expos and pop-up voting through interviews and exit interviews. The interview scripts are shown in Appendix B (for expos) and Appendix C (for voting

D. Williams and D. Waisanen, *Real Money, Real Power?*,
https://doi.org/10.1007/978-3-030-59201-1_6

locations). A total of 78 interviews were conducted at project expos (12) and pop-up voting locations (66). We recorded these interviews on data forms and, with participant permission, with audio recordings.[1]

The research assistants reported sparse attendance and, in several instances, difficulty locating project expos. The objective of this data collection was to learn public knowledge about participatory budgeting at this stage, the effect of lobbying on votes, and the degree to which this population is engaged in the process. Notably, several voting locations were associated with project proposals and the volunteers at one of the observed voting locations were behind a table with a poster promoting a project associated with the voting location. These conditions provide considerable advantage to projects related to the projects, thereby suggesting a bias. Advocates of competing projects may perceive disadvantages and, even if they do not perceive it, they may experience disadvantages. Such bias stands in direct opposition to an important objective of participatory democracy to increase the legitimacy of governance. Table 6.1 shows the results to questions regarding participants' PB meeting attendance.

The gap between those present at this stage and those who hadn't, and couldn't, attend earlier meetings due to barriers was striking. In these results, we see PB as a hodgepodge of stages involving different people and interests. Table 6.1 shows an analysis of survey questions about attending meetings. Of these 78 respondents, only 15 were able to attend neighborhood assemblies to propose ideas. Of the 63 non-attendees, 53 were unable to attend for the predominant reason (60%) that they were unaware of the process (84% of those who offered a reason).[2] For the remaining 10, there were time constraints, such as, "I've got a kindergartner, I'm a single mom, so yeah, and a full-time job." Marginalized people may be unable to be delegates. Across our research, there was plenty of talk about considering the interests of the underserved, but the discussion was balanced against the further assertion that the government should serve everyone, not just the marginalized.

[1] A research assistant with technical difficulties produced no usable recordings. We have 53 total transcripts, since the assistant who had technical difficulties had 21 interviews. Of the 57 usable interviews, four were not recorded, two by error and with two declines. Our research assistant did have paper records, however, that are included in this chapter's tables.

[2] The survey allowed open-ended responses. Fifteen provided no specific reason.

Table 6.1 Meeting attendance

Q4 [For districts where there was an idea-collection meeting] Were you able to attend the idea-collection meetings this year?

Y	N
15	63
19%	81%

Q5 [If no] Do you have a time constraint, such as a job or family commitment, that prevented you from attending the idea-collection meeting?

Y	N	Not aware	Family	Working	Work and family	Was away	Family and school	Other conflict	Yes	Total
53	9	32	2	2	1	1	0	0	15	53
85%	15%	60%	4%	4%	2%	2%	0%	0%	28%	100%

Q6 Were you able to participate as a budget delegate this year?

Y	N
9	69
12%	88%

Q7 [If no] Do you have a time constraint, such as a job or family commitment, that prevents you from being a budget delegate?

Y	N	Not aware	Family	Working	Work and family	Was away	Family and school	Other conflict	Yes	Total
53	13	29	0	3	0	0	1	2	17	52[a]
80%	20%	56%	0%	6%	0%	0%	2%	4%	33%	100%

[a]There was one nonresponse

The actualization of this admonition to consider the marginalized, could not be observed because of the lack of transparency. In any case, acting on behalf of the marginalized may not have the same effect as allowing them voice. The projects recommended in the six neighborhood assemblies for which there are data are not clearly reflective of any marginalized population, unless being school age is treated as de facto marginalization. Substantially marginalized populations of New York City at this time include such groups as homeless people, addicted drug users, single parents, minimum wage earners, and the chronically unemployed. It is not clear why any of the projects shown in Table 4.1 would benefit these marginalized groups. Only 9 respondents were able to be budget delegates (5 of these were interviewed at project expos, accounting for 38% of respondents at expos). For non-attendees, 29 (56%) were unaware of the meetings (76% of those who offered a reason). Table 6.2 lists further variables of relevance.

Table 6.2 shows an analysis of respondents' suggestion of projects for participatory budgeting and their subsequent success. Eight of the nine respondents (89%) who were delegates suggested projects and all (100%) of their suggested projects were subsequently found on the ballots. Seven of the 69 non-delegates (10%) suggested projects and two (29%) of their projects were subsequently found on the ballots. Although the delegates were 20% of the respondents, they suggested 53% of the respondents' proposed projects and 80% of those that were subsequently found on the ballots. Table 6.2 also shows that 34% of the respondents have engaged in participatory budgeting in previous years, including eight of the nine delegates (89%) and 26% of the non-delegates. Twenty of these respondents had a project selected by PB including 7 delegates (78%) and 19% of the non-delegates. Eight respondents said that their projects had been completed, while two said they had not. One expected the project to be completed soon, while eight were not sure and there was one nonresponse. Twelve (15%) of the respondents had been asked to vote for a particular project; however, most of their qualitative responses indicate these requests were family or friends.

There are two particularly noteworthy implications from Table 6.2, confirming much of what we learned about in the prior stage (see Chapter 4): (1) delegates were advocates of specific projects, not just engaged community members who wanted to do the right thing, and (2) delegates were extremely successful in getting their projects onto the ballot. All of the delegates who advocated a project got it onto the ballot,

Table 6.2 Suggested projects, prior year participation, and vote advocacy

			Yes examined			
	Yes	*No*	*Delegate*	*Share of all delegates*	*Not delegate*	*Share of all non-delegates*
Q8 Have you suggested any projects this year?	15	61	8	89%	7	10%
	20%	80%				
Share suggestions by Delegates/Non-Delegates			53%		47%	
Q9 Is your project represented among the ones shown here in the Expo? On the ballot?	10	5	8	89%	2	3%
	67%	6%				
Share on ballot that are suggested by Delegates/Non-Delegates			80%		20%	
Share suggested on ballot			100%		29%	
Q14 Have you engaged in PB in earlier years?[a]	26	51	8	89%	18	26%
	34%	66%				
Q15 Have any of your preferred projects been selected in previous years?[a]	20 77%	6 23%	7	78%	13	19%
	Yes	No	Other response[b]			
Q16 [If yes] Have any of those projects been completely implemented?[a]	8 40%	2 10%	10 50%			
Q10 Other than responding to you while viewing a poster, have you been asked to vote for a project?	12 15%	65 83%	1 1%			

[a]There were 1-2 nonresponses to Q10, Q15, and Q16

[b]For Q16 other responses were "not sure," "think so," "will be soon," "don't think," "can't recall," and "don't know"

whereas 5/7th of non-delegates failed to get their project onto the ballot. It is further noteworthy that most (8/9) of the delegates are seasoned PB participants, as compared with the other respondents, of whom only a quarter make up this category. The vote solicitation data generally reflects a lack of vote promoting behavior; we had generally anticipated that there might be such behavior.

In the end, experts tend to narrow the range of projects that community members can obtain through participatory budgeting. This is one of the ways by which the participants' power is limited rather than released. A second limitation, observed in one council district, was the conduct of neighborhood assemblies that were generally restricted to predetermined service categories.

More significantly, power is produced through voice, which we define as being present during critical decision-making phases of the participatory budget. As shown in Table 6.2, delegates are much more likely to get their suggested projects on the ballot than are other members of the community. These observations are consistent with Shybalkina (2019), who reports that delegates engage in PB as advocates of particular projects.

Personal Benefits and Legitimacy

At this stage, we were especially privy to the personal and professional benefits at stake. With the PB cycle narrowing to the actual voting and selection phase, the intentions of participants came plainly into view. Some of our interview questions sought qualitative responses revealing the nature of participants' different motivations. Four of the interview questions sought qualitative responses, such as "Q11 [If asked to vote for a particular project] What did the person asking you to vote for a project say?" There were only a few responses to this question, but they were telling.

Some responses mentioned advocates, generally reflecting school system based advocacy. One person told us "the school that my daughter's in, the PTA there is very, very active, so that's the reason I wanted to vote." We learned that an "administrator at a child's school asked to vote for renovation of [a] bathroom – repeatedly, asked parents to please vote." Some mentioned family members or friends: "My wife said basically I should vote for things that are basically close to us," like voting for a tree. In a conversation with a friend this came up and one person said, "you know the tree guards are a good buy." So this participant responded, "Yeah, but good luck with that, because if that even goes to [inaudible], every kid, every parent, everybody.' … But I was already going to vote for [the] tree guard." This respondent is saying that because there is a big push in the schools, nonschool items as obscure as tree guards are not likely to be approved. This demonstrates the diversity of items suggested by advocates of particular projects.

For Q13 we asked "How did you make your vote selection?"[3] Many responses were either mixed or focused on personal or professional benefit. One person said they were there "Selfishly, for the park here, for safety, and for school." Similarly, we heard "There was at least one project that cut close to me." A participant mentioned, "I think that, you know, given the opportunity to vote I think I voted for the things that I think would impact where I live and the way I go about my, you know, [my life]." Another shared, "I work in education, so I wanted something, and I'm a mom, so sort of think about education facilities and also children." One participant said, "I am an educator and so, I usually tend to vote for education related items and candidates and that was really the thing that guided me most voting today."[4] In terms of issues, we also heard about, "Two which were of personal interest. One was that it's the science. Anything that forwards science, I'd be for." One's immediate circle also came into play, as in one person sharing how, "Based on what I personally would like to see and based on the limits that we have to choose from. Yeah, my own preference and preferences of the people I know."

On a brighter note, despite all the variation observed, we still saw a lot of civic and social mindedness exhibited about all this from many participants—reinforcing the importance of the equity and inclusion theme already highlighted at several junctures. Responses to this question focused on the general benefit to an area or the benefits for needy individuals. One person said, "I made the selection based on the five that I thought would be more beneficial to the area, community." We heard, "And the last one I voted for was the elevator lift ... to help people

[3] Question 12, asked only at Expos, was a lead into a qualitative question. In other words, between Q11 and Q13, there was a question that is asked at Expos, but not asked at voting sites. At expos, Q13 was asked only of those who have made a vote selection (Q12). At vote sites, the interview was after the vote, so all respondents made a selection.

[4] There was also some resistance to the perceived over-focus on schools from another participant: "I don't think there's an easy answer for that. I tend to focus more on the non-school projects just 'cause I know in this district a lot of people are voting and I don't have kids so I feel like you know let me focus on the other stuff." There was also some focus on perceived economic utility: "I voted on what sounded like the best way to spend the money."

with [a] disability, I think is important." Similarly, one person reported how, "I wanted to disperse the budget possibilities within different neighborhoods, and split them between housing, playgrounds, and other resources, so fair distribution." Additionally, these motives were based "on what I thought was important to the community, such as schools and veterans. Because veterans, they fight our wars and whatever. And, better education leads to better leaders for tomorrow." Despite so many areas that need to be improved upon, PB still does important work in either providing the civically minded an opportunity to express their values, or in bringing more civic-mindedness to a community.

In fact, much legitimacy was accorded to PB. Q17 asked, "How satisfied or dissatisfied are you with the PB project(s) for this year? In past years? Why?" Most participants, including those who expressed a substantial lack of knowledge about the PB process in response to questions 4 through 7, expressed satisfaction in response to this one: "I'm fairly satisfied, yeah. ... I think it's a diverse group of projects. I think the process has opened up for the public options and selections and I think it's more transparent." Another said they were "Satisfied. They seemed legitimate to me. ... All just sort of things that make sense to improve." We heard that "I think it is a good spread of choices. It seems to be good," and "I think they're all good projects that there is a need for." One person concluded, "I think it's great that a community have choice and a little power in how to spend the money of the city budget." This last comment should be very encouraging for those participatory democracy advocates who view this process as producing legitimacy for governance. However, it does not settle the question whether legitimacy is genuine or manipulated. From all of our preceding data, much of PB skews in the latter direction, despite its adherents' very good intentions.

Not everyone was happy with the process or choices. One respondent said, "I'm kind of lukewarm because we submitted a lot of good ideas and the city agencies, because of their protocols, knocked them out. ... So we ended up with ... We started out with 10 that were submitted for vetting with the city agencies in one committee and ended up with three." Here the influence of city agencies was once again on full display. Cost considerations loomed large, as another shared how, "because the costs keep rising every year. Two years ago to fix a ... you know repave the basketball court and fix the rim [it] costs 350,000 [dollars]. Now it costs like 700,000 [dollars]. I mean that's ridiculous." Similarly, a participant shared: "I like the ideas; the budgets seem astronomical. I don't understand why it would take that much money to make what they are saying. So, that's shocking." These remarks do not demonstrate that the cost estimates are incorrect, but they are evidence that they are not transparent. Again, assigning costs can also be a way of making sure some items are either on or off the agenda (i.e., if you don't want it, price high, if you do want it, price low). Given this potential, the stakes for transparency are even higher—and support the idea that PB in the U.S. is mostly top-down and consultative.

To get further clarity, we searched the websites of the most likely agencies to find PB cost estimates, the Independent Budget Office and the City Comptroller. These websites have no reports on participatory budgeting. An email communication from the Independent Budget Office reports that that office has not completed any relevant analysis. An inquiry with the City Comptroller never received a response. The available evidence strongly suggests that the participatory budgeting cost estimation process is not transparent. This may allow additional discretion to the agency experts. Regardless of whether it does, it has the potential of undermining the common participatory democracy concern of legitimizing governance.

Others hesitated in response to Q17 due to a lack of knowledge or because they only had minor complaints. One person said simply, "I have no opinion." Another, "I'm satisfied. I think it was a nice range of different choices. Of course, it made it harder to pick sometimes, in some ways. ... It was nicer that way because I felt like last year, I won't say it was narrow, but it was much more focused in certain ways" and, "I like that it, there were more choices. If environmental stuff appealed to you, there was options there. If community minded stuff was there, that appealed to me too and also different age groups. One thing that I was sad that I didn't see anything for this year was the seniors because there were things for seniors last year."

Some picked apart the choices from previous years. One person mentioned, "There was one in years past that I felt that was not worthy. ... It was decorative lighting for the West Village." Last, one person mentioned how "I really can't judge because I don't know what other options would be, but I think they're fine, yes I like the general tenor of them, just that they're very community oriented and they seem to help people who need it." Overall, in political matters a range of agreements and disagreements are to be expected. But what's most interesting about

PB processes is not necessarily the varying degrees of legitimacy perceived by respondents, but the way in which decisions are actually reached across the annual cycle. The picture is largely one of personal and professional benefits in practice, toward which beliefs about legitimacy can end up meaning very little.

Delivery and Tokenism

At this PB stage, many of the themes that surfaced in prior rounds manifest across our interviews. Additional considerations concerned the problems with delivering on what was voted on—what's the use of voting for projects if they don't become reality, after all—and a belief that PB can have tokenisitic qualities, offering lip service to democracy but seldom helping citizens realize it. Q18 of our interviews asked "What have we not discussed that you think is important for understanding the process of how PB decisions are made?" There were comments about the failure of government to deliver these capital projects in the first place: "I still think that's important. [I'm] kind of disappointed in the Department of Education that they don't just go ahead and do that." The respondent communicated that small capital projects should be part of the ordinary planning process. For example, if a school needs a bathroom repaired, they should just do it and not have to wait for city council intervention. This comment can also be considered in the context of the projects enumerated in Table 4.1. Many of these projects reflect the basic performance of governmental functions. If a school needs a bathroom repair, playground work, or technology upgraded in a $28 billion Department of Education Budget (with an additional $3.6 billion in unspent capital funds), it stands to reason that it should be able to repair bathrooms, upgrade technology, and schedule playground work within a reasonable amount of time. These basic needs should not be deferred until such time as a city council member commits funds out of a paltry $5 million annual discretionary fund while that council member is considering numerous other weighty needs.

Of particular concern was the black hole that projects became in terms of pricing and vendors, a concern repeatedly raised throughout this project: "I think when you talk about the money, [crosstalk] a lot of procedure we don't know. So, you put the money in, so how much money go into the vendor? The supplier, so [crosstalk] itemize how they spend the money. We only see the money go to them." Similarly, one person said, "Well, I don't know. There was one project that was actually down the block from me and I wanted to vote for it because it's about a park and it's about the pathways. They wanted to redo the pathways. Because they are uneven and I've tripped a couple times. But the estimate was $620,000. I thought that was outrageous because it's only a very small thing that they're doing." Some see PB pricing and delivery as a kind of sausage factory where so much about *how* things really get done is beyond reach: "I think when you talk about the money, [crosstalk] a lot of procedure we don't know. So, you put the money in, so how much money go into the vendor? The supplier, so [crosstalk] itemize how they spend the money. We only see the money go to them." Expressing skepticism about the real money and real power asserted by PB, another shared, "I would love to see even more participatory budget as far as the budget percentage of the whole budget that we have for the district. That would be lovely." And citizens' concerns are valid on both cost projections and delivery. If there were sources on the process for estimates, more trust in this part of PB might be garnered. Yet, we are aware of nothing more than anecdotes that suggest that agencies eyeball projects or use preset estimates for project types, with no specifics of the actual projects. We personally doubt the validity of some of the costs we have seen and other finance people we have discussed this issue with are also skeptical.

One of the key problems with the delivery of PB concerns the entire decision-making process itself. At this late stage, citizens are expected to enact a process that to many still hasn't been clear to that point. Suggesting preferential treatment, one respondent told us:

> I don't think that it is very [clear] how the decisions are made in terms of how people come up with the ideas. I know that there is some lobbying, because I was part of the PB, I was a delegate last year, so there is some lobbying happening. So, something is given an advantage by knowing about it and bringing a delegate who will support and push the project, and I'm sure there are many other programs that are not aware of that. I think more awareness across the board, so people in different groups would know about it and be able to advocate the projects. I don't think that it has very big visibility, even here in this neighborhood.

The point is that those who know to participate are the ones who get the benefit. Participants also expressed concern for "Just how are these projects nominated" and, in a running theme across all the stages, how

"I think there needs to be more transparency, and just overall publicity of the process. If you're not already tuned into a council's email system, then how are you going to know?" Across the interviews, there was a sense that citizens were delivering on something that was not well known, nor that what would be delivered by others beyond these decisions would be communicated about to a satisfactory degree.

So many of these project expo and pop-up voting remarks centered on PB's messaging that it's worth drawing attention to the responses we gathered. One participant shared, "I think more publicity about it, prior to it and this meeting, would be helpful. And somehow, to prove to me that this really works, would be good." Again, concerns about delivery were especially pronounced during this stage, likely since it was much closer to implementation than the earlier stages in September through December, in which the actualities of PB could seem far away. Another person said, "How it will be communicated, I guess I could have gotten an email maybe looking at something more broad-based from the mayor, or our local assembly men," while we additionally heard, "I think it should be maybe more public awareness of where these things happen, because I was totally unaware, so I happened to be walking by was like, 'Oh, okay. I kind of heard about that because I've read the Metro the other day,' but other than that, I didn't know much else, so it's my first time engaging in PB." We also heard that those connected to PB should "Make it more accessible. This is the first time [I'm] seeing a voting location. [They] should help people know about it." Additionally, "To me, I think it's just more of a getting the word out more, than the whole process. It's more about kind of, advertising when the votes are and the issues, and the actual issues themselves."

Some participants had a noteworthy ambivalence about PB's potential tokenism. While drawn to the democratic ideals of the initiative, an overriding sense that the gap between these ideals and the actual processes and products of PB was too wide. One person said, "[I] Like the idea, it's nice. I worry it just favors the connected. Families with kids who get email or those who go to the farmer's market [the location of this interview]. Rich liberal guilt. I like participating in democracy. I think it's cool. I'm glad I ran into the [table where the votes were collected]. It took two sources of awareness to get me to do it." Another participant questioned the point of PB in similar terms:

> I sort of just feel like PB is sort of this feel good kind of token democracy thing. They're all good projects. I don't really know how it materially matters, if it's us voting for it or some ... [inaudible] is choosing it or something. I don't know. It sort of feels like ... it's good if it makes people more about getting more civically engaged, but I don't know if it does. A lot of people ... I think people, they want to tune out people who are trying to get something from them. ... I'm guess I'm sort of saying ... I sort of think it's a token thing that doesn't really matter, but I also think it's a good thing. I'm guess I'm sort of saying ... I sort of think it's a token thing that doesn't really matter, but I also think it's a good thing.

Most critical to this participant's comment is the back and forth about PB's value. As we've tried to recognize throughout this project, there are aspects of PB certainly worth praising and, in its most general tenets toward including more people in democratic decision-making about taxpayer monies, it's wholly to be commended. At the same time, this participant can't shake the notion that in its current iterations, if PB hasn't gone awry, then there's simply too much opportunity for it to go awry absent better accountability, transparency, and other applied criteria.

Slipping Between the Cracks

Beyond the questions asked at the expo and voting interviews, one final element we should draw attention toward concerns the central issue at stake in this book: what is it like to be a citizen navigating PB processes at this stage? In our notes, several observations were made with bearing upon our research question regarding if citizens have the real money and real power PB claims. This category is best summed up as concerning a number of issues where citizens' interests—and, as a consequence, the public interest—fall through the cracks.

A notable lack of citizens' presence and influence occurred across many of these events. The following observer notes documenting the interview process provides some insight: "Last night I was at an Astoria location for 30 minutes before anyone from the Councilmember's office even showed up (I got there at 6[pm] when they were supposed to), and not a soul came to vote during the 90 minutes they were there." In fact, one of our assistants noted how, "It could be due to online voting or just bad luck, but several of the locations we've selected have been total ghost towns."

We also observed many appeals to citizens that, quite simply, fell on deaf ears. We observed a council member and staff recruiting PB voters from otherwise disinterested individuals. While the effort seems admirable, it nevertheless shows a lack of community awareness of PB: "At the [Stuyvesant Town] community center now. [The council member] is here with his staff going up to elderly bridge players and explaining to each what PB is." Our assistants noted that a number of informal and implicit qualities guided PB in practice (which are worth attending to at a granular level in improving the initiative as a whole):

> I am beginning to understand that time of day, day of the week and type of voting location have the greatest effects on catching PB voters. Unfortunately, weekdays during the day seem to be the worst time to catch people. ... I anticipate that we may need to hit multiple voting sites simultaneously this weekend in order to complete the ... surveys. Locations that already have a lot of foot traffic (i.e., farmer[']s markets) would probably be the only way to encounter a sufficient number of PB voters. Of course, weather may also play a role. The biggest obstacle has not been getting people to agree to do the survey, but rather encountering enough people who are coming to vote. And within those who just voted most had never heard of PB prior to voting.
>
> I'm currently at 12 responses after visiting four districts. Two of those districts did not yield any responses. ... [I] just now went to a Constatinides voting site (the district office). The staff there were helpful but did suggest that online voting had greatly diminished foot traffic for PB vote week (I was told that more than half now vote online),[5] and typically only 3-4 people stop by to vote all day! Sure enough, I waited downstairs for nearly an hour and not a single person came to vote. I decided to cut my losses and will head over to another district with a different type of location (a library).

All of this suggests there are ample opportunities for citizens' interest in and presence for PB to slip between the cracks of these systemic and event-based considerations. Its challenges are often monumental.

Also associated with the voting process, a partial list of voting locations is shown in Appendix D. As with other information, this list could be compiled only by contacting council offices. This list includes schools,

[5] This could seem like an argument for making online voting completely the norm. Yet we believe that online voting advantages the comparative elite. This is a subject of concern at the citywide advisory meetings. I see it as an argument that the relatively disadvantaged do not know about PB.

libraries, community centers, and parks, which were, in some cases, potential beneficiaries of specific PB proposals. Locations at which the first author interviewed included at least two city facilities that were potential beneficiaries of PB funding on the ballots. At one of those locations, the pop-up voting table was staffed by volunteers who represented the organization promoting a project.

We also engaged in post-observation data collection that brought up other issues, one of which is especially egregious and is in apparent violation of the city's open data laws. The research team downloaded 479 documents of ideas (approximately 479 distinct ideas, but some documents had multiple ideas) from two idea posting websites, http://ideas.pbnyc.org/ and https://pbnyc39.com/idea-collection/; such sites are referred to as an "idea map" (New York City Council, 2020). One of these websites is managed by a single council member, while the other reflected all engaged council districts. For the broader one, we sought the underlying geocoded dataset to compare suggestions with subsequent ballots, but it was never supplied.

The first solicitation was in August 2019, and failure to supply it is in ostensible defilement of the city's open data laws. We contacted each council office and asked them to describe how the ideas were used in the decision-making process, and how they get from idea maps to the delegate decision-making. Out of 29 offices contacted, only seven provided a response—indicating, once again, how there are transparency problems around participatory budgeting. The general nature of the response is that spreadsheets are referred to the council office, which then eliminates ineligible projects and refers them along with other ideas such as idea cards to the committee chair. Some council offices may refer all ideas to delegates, leaving it to them to eliminate clearly ineligible projects. The use by committee chairs was not described. From our observations, the committee chairs briefly review the larger idea set without enthusiasm, then turn to the real agenda, the ideas promoted by the delegates.

One responding council office was able to identify one proposal from the idea map that got to the ballot. Notes from one call says: "Council office gets sheet from speaker's office, no idea how many from website (in past cycles or in general), delegates rank order ideas. Says nothing is stopping delegates from pushing their own ideas or getting friends to also volunteer." And this is where citizens face their greatest challenges with PB: between the cracks, there are too many opportunities for closed-door decision-making, a lining up of the usual suspects to vote on preferred, partial projects, and ultimately introducing a potential expectation that the system can be gamed.

In the concluding chapter, we cover the implications and extensions of this project for future work on PB. In the ultimate hope of helping PB improve and spread, by addressing many of the glaring issues revealed in this book we underscore both the theoretical and practical actions that might be taken.

References

New York City Council. (2020). *Participatory budgeting*. Retrieved from https://council.nyc.gov/pb/.

Shybalkina, I. (2019). Designing citizen participation processes to help people make more reasoned choices. In I. Shybalkina (Ed.), *Engagement-equity trade-off: A mixed-methods study of participatory budgeting and property tax assessment appeals in large US cities* (Dissertation). Draft chapter with shared info.

CHAPTER 7

Conclusion: Doing Participatory Budgeting Right

Abstract The conclusion offers four implications and three recommendations for better participatory budgeting practice. First we note how, rather than reflecting a coordinated participatory budgeting process, each council district operates its own process that reflects that there as many PB projects as there are participating council members. Second, there is substantial top-down behavior that effectively inhibits sharing power with marginalized members of the community. Third, the process is opaque in many ways, with many members of the community unaware of participatory budgeting. There is a lack of public notice with respect to the critical agenda setting stage. Fourth, some voting locations are potential beneficiaries of proposed projects and some volunteers at pop-up voting tables are advocates for particular projects, which undermines the fairness of process. Proposed changes to improve participatory budgeting include taking positive steps to invite in disadvantaged members of the community, create a reliable normalized process, eliminate opaque practices, and detach participatory budgeting from the council discretionary budget. We urge all involved with PB to address the barriers detailed in this book, to keep reaching toward the higher, critically important goals it has set forth throughout the world, and in doing so, truly offer citizens the real money and real power they deserve.

Keywords Diversity · Awareness · Advocacy · Barriers · Agency

D. Williams and D. Waisanen, *Real Money, Real Power?*,
https://doi.org/10.1007/978-3-030-59201-1_7

Right as we were finishing this book, just about every society across the world was hit by the largest crisis in several generations: the global pandemic COVID-19. Economies were shut down, people all over the planet were forced to quarantine inside for weeks and months on end, and uncertainty filled the air. It's also been a time when the force of governments to serve their citizens well or poorly has been focused in a way that we had never seen before. Where an initiative like PB may previously have been seen as a nice add on to the work of government and its citizenry, during and after COVID-19 many have realized that such matters are essential. When one's income and life hang in the balance of government decision-making, sometimes reflecting but too often diverting from all citizens' interests, the need for inclusive, equitable, and most of all, efficient and effective means of government distributions are a must.

This project has offered readers a glimpse, from multiple methods and angles, of the fissures of PB from citizens' vantage points. Through observations, interviews, and examinations of media and other forms of research, we took an everyday perspective of PB. Overall, PB deserves much praise for what it is trying to do—enacting democratic budgets that reflect citizens' concerns. But at the level of everyday life, the current version of it, as practiced in NYC, is so filled with fractures, disconnections, and a lack of transparency over too many of its moving parts, that some serious work needs to be done to make it all work better. We began and will end on that note. We're looking to not simply be critical, but to make the next iterations of PB work much better than they currently do, in the hopes that practitioners, scholars, and others involved with PB can do it right. This concluding section highlights four implications and three recommendations from our analyses.[1]

As mentioned throughout this project, first, there is no singular PB project in New York City. Instead, there are numerous PB projects, as many as there are council members who engage in the practice. This is incredibly problematic for many reasons. Chief among them is that if citizens are offered the promise of "real money and real power," that money and power is not equitably distributed to begin with. It shouldn't be the case that one council district has exacting processes for rolling out PB's general tenets and processes, while another undergoes lax organization with confusing messaging and little opportunities for citizen input.

[1] Note that these summarizing remarks likely apply to some or many, but not all of the practices found in each of the districts.

Second, too many actors and agencies with special interests and top-down forms of involvement limit the capacities of citizens to exercise democratic power in PB. In this study, we examined the power transferred especially to marginalized or underserved populations and looked for evidence of clientelism, interest group behavior, and expert influence. We discovered many additional concerns about transparency. There is moderate evidence of clientelism in that the very nature of the resource allocation by council direction is a form of clientelism, particularly in that the sorts of projects funded by this process appear to reflect a failure to create a consistent, rational process for meeting many of these needs through the ordinary operation of government. As the types of projects selected and the nature of participation does not show a significant redirection of resources to marginalized populations, the process can better be viewed as a refinement of clientelistic practices, the essential feature of which is to keep the council member in a visible role delivering these resources to the constituency.

We found little evidence of interest group behavior, but substantial evidence of expert influence. Experts participate as members of the neighborhood and also constrain choices in the project validation process. In some instances, experts also use their role in the consultative process to lobby for projects they prefer or to veto those they do not. The lack of transparency in expert involvement leads to distrust among some participants, both with respect to the narrowing of participant choice and the cost estimation process. The lack of transparency around budget estimates also bodes poorly for citizen participation—expected costs come out of thin air and could be a way of exerting each expert's own opinions of what's worthy and what's not in assignments. At the same time, the overriding influence—both perceived and real—of government agencies looms large over the PB budgeting processes of which we partook. There's an expectation that agencies will say no to projects outside their scope, that are either too small or too large, and that cost attributions will come out of thin air, with little competitive influence.

Third, poor messaging and a variety of other factors make PB opaque and subject to the influence of advocates who, beyond generating ideas and exploring choices in the deliberative fashion that PB idolizes, instead come to various stages of the PB process with preset interests or narrow personal, professional, or organizational benefits in mind. As discussed throughout this report, PBNYC lacks transparency. There is no centralized source of meeting schedules or locations. There is limited public notice of neighborhood assemblies using constituent service modes in most districts, but also news media in a few. Still, of the 53 interviews at expos and voting locations who said they did not attend a neighborhood assembly the dominant reason (60%) was that they had not heard about it. A troubling lack of transparency is found with the budget delegate process, in particular. There is no public notice of the delegate meetings and, at least in some districts, they are not open to the public. There is evidence that the delegates choose to be delegates because they are advocates for projects and that they have sufficient discretion with the delegate process to place these projects on the ballot. Projects for which there is no delegate-advocate receive very limited, if any consideration, for the ballot.

At least some council members deem these meetings as closed; 56% of interview respondents said they were unaware of these meetings. The lack of transparency in delegate meetings is compounded by both the limiting and ambiguous direction given in delegate training, where delegates are admonished to consider the underserved, but not to forget that many government programs should benefit everyone. They are also required to narrow the list of ballot items to a very small number, not large enough to include all the valid projects, leaving it unclear how some valid projects are to be cut. These vague requirements combined with the overrepresentation of project advocates among the delegates suggest substantial opportunity for preferential treatment of the advocates' projects.[2]

Fourth, this discussion would not be complete without a brief word on the implicit bias associated with voting locations and the use of volunteer voting staff who are advocates of particular projects. It should be assumed that users of facilities that have a stake in the participatory budgeting process are more likely to vote for resources for those facilities. Using such places as voting locations substantially advantages those facilities in comparison with other facilities that have proposals on the ballot. More so, the use of advocates to staff the pop-up voting locations provides a substantial advantage to their projects.

Based on this study, we recommend that the participatory budgeting process be substantially reformed in three major ways. One step would be to provide voice to the marginalized. Simply keeping the disadvantaged in mind while making decisions is not sufficient. To provide voice requires outreach into environments where the marginalized can

[2] This is strongly suggested by the results in Table 6.2.

be found,[3] inviting them into the participatory budgeting process and possibly compensating them for their resource commitment, assisting them to understand and participate, and arranging for an adequate share of the process to occur at a time and place and in a manner that accommodates their capacities.

A next major improvement should involve making the norms and processes for participatory budgeting far more uniform and centralized. If the program is administered in the same way, with the same expectations, across all jurisdictions, the opportunity to be involved will build the type of equity and inclusion that citizens clearly want to see operating in these situations. Administering PB in this fashion will require some needed oversight and accountability so that citizens' experiences can be aligned across areas. Without more uniform standards and practices, participatory budgeting can turn into a hodgepodge of different, confusing processes, and will continue to remain unaccountable to publics beyond experts and more.

Along these lines, we also recommend a thorough commitment to transparency. At a minimum, this would involve centralizing and better communicating the schedules of neighborhood meetings and delegate meetings. The practice of closed delegate meetings should be entirely eliminated. It would also be beneficial to develop a more inclusive method of recruiting and selecting delegates and holding meetings in a manner that is accessible to the marginalized.

Last, the project cost estimation practices should be made transparent. Two methods for doing this would be (1) to produce itemized cost estimates in much the same manner as a bid and (2) to periodically audit a sample of completed projects to compare actual expenditures with estimates.

We also recommend that the process be detached from the city council discretionary budget. It is difficult to envision a version of participatory budgeting attached to the discretionary budget that is not generally focused on showing that the council member is delivering for the voters, which also involves withholding rational program design so that the delivery is possible.

[3] During this study we have observed that the council do outreach to various language groups that may be marginalized. Many council members account for Spanish and Chinese. Some council members may include other languages.

At the end of the day, PB holds too important a promise for citizens, one that has taken too long across many societies to realize. Since government budgeting matters have been some of the least engaged aspects of civic life, but affect just about every citizen in more profound ways than often recognized, budgets should not be at the sole discretion of powerful individuals, representatives, or special interests. Enter PB, offering the ability for citizens to take back control of some of their own money, and more importantly, signaling that everyone's voice should matter in material and social allocations. Yet to truly realize that promise in practice, we need to continue seeing all the real ways that the initiatives and events around PB actually play out on the ground. We urge all involved with PB to address the barriers detailed in this book, to keep reaching toward the higher, critically important goals it has set forth throughout the world, and in doing so, truly offer citizens the real money and real power they deserve.

Appendix A: Methods Overview

This study was conducted without collaboration with any entity that promotes or implements participatory budgeting. The objective of the project was specifically to observe the experience of those who are not insiders.

The study was conducted through mixed methods. In the first phase we engaged in passive participant observation. A primary researcher and two graduate research assistants attended seven neighborhood assemblies (idea-generating meetings), two budget delegate training meetings, and one budget delegate meeting. Although we attended these meetings, we did not make suggestions or engage in any decision-making processes. The neighborhood assemblies were open public meetings, so we did not announce ourselves at the meetings, although we did reveal our role when asked. After attending the delegate training meetings, we were told that the delegate meetings were closed, and had substantial difficulty accessing them after revising our human subjects application to reflect this condition. Contemporaneous photos, notes, and transcripts of these meetings were used to prepare this report.

Stymied by the denial of access to delegate meetings, the second phase consisted of making a very broad search for online postings about participatory budgeting, searching for hyper-local news media in New York through Google, and searching Facebook posts, Twitter feeds, and council member websites. Ultimately we obtained 1,295 online news media observations and 297 council communications. The council

D. Williams and D. Waisanen, *Real Money, Real Power?*,
https://doi.org/10.1007/978-3-030-59201-1

communications through Facebook and Twitter extended over several to many years and contained numerous individual observations. These data were analyzed specifically by looking at descriptions of participant and budget delegate experiences, while examining the transparency of the budget delegate process.

In the third phase, we conducted interviews at budget expo meetings (where advocates of particular projects presented information about their projects to members of the public) and at pop-up voting locations. We obtained a total of 78 interviews. The interview included quantitative (yes/no) questions and qualitative (open-ended) questions. The quantitative data are reported in descriptive tables in this book. The qualitative data are analyzed in the same manner as other qualitative data reported.

Although not a phase, we also report on researcher experiences throughout this process. Particularly significant are the experiences related to obtaining information about participatory budgeting events and unexpected observations at pop-up voting locations.

Appendix B: Script for 10-Minute Interviews at Expo Locations

1. [Record identifier]
2. Hi, I'm a researcher at the City University of New York. Would you have 10 minutes to discuss your views of the participatory budgeting process? Our goal is to better understand how decisions are made. We can offer a $10 gift card for your time, but agreeing or disagreeing to the interview is completely voluntary and, while we will use our results in published research, we are not recording names or identifying anyone who participates in this research. Would you be interested in sharing your views in a quick interview?
3. [If yes] May I record the interview?
4. [For districts where there was an idea-collection meeting] Were you able to attend the idea-collection meetings this year?
5. [If no] Do you have a time constraint, such as a job or family commitment, that prevented you from attending the idea-collection meeting?
6. Were you able to participate as a budget delegate this year?
7. [If no] Do you have a time constraint, such as a job or family commitment, that prevents you from being a budget delegate?
8. Have you suggested any projects this year?
9. [If yes] Is your project represented among the ones shown here in the Expo?

D. Williams and D. Waisanen, *Real Money, Real Power?*,
https://doi.org/10.1007/978-3-030-59201-1

10. Other than responding to you while viewing a poster, have you been asked to vote for a project?
11. [If yes] What did the person asking you to vote for a project say?
12. Have you selected a project or projects to vote for?
13. [If yes] How did you make that selection?
14. Have you engaged in PB in earlier years?
15. Have any of your preferred projects been selected in previous years?
16. [If yes] Have any of those projects been completely implemented?
17. How satisfied or dissatisfied are you with the PB project(s) for this year? In past years? Why?
18. What have we not discussed that you think is important for understanding the process of how PB decisions are made?

Appendix C: Script for 10-Minute Interviews at Voting Locations

1. [Record identifier]
2. Hi, I'm a researcher at the City University of New York. Would you have 10 minutes to discuss your views of the participatory budgeting process? Our goal is to better understand how decisions are made. We can offer a $10 gift card for your time, but agreeing or disagreeing to the interview is completely voluntary and, while we will use our results in published research, we are not recording names or identifying anyone who participates in this research. Would you be interested in sharing your views in a quick interview?
3. May I record the interview?
4. [For districts where there was an idea-collection meeting] Were you able to attend the idea-collection meetings this year?
5. [If no] Do you have a time constraint, such as a job or family commitment, that prevented you from attending the idea-collection meeting?
6. Were you able to participate as a budget delegate this year?
7. [If no] Do you have a time constraint, such as a job or family commitment, that prevents you from being a budget delegate?
8. Have you suggested any projects this year?
9. [If yes] Was your project included among the ones shown on the ballot?
10. Has anyone asked you to vote for a project?

D. Williams and D. Waisanen, *Real Money, Real Power?*,
https://doi.org/10.1007/978-3-030-59201-1

11. [If yes] What did that person say?
12. [Have you selected, not asked of those who have already voted.]
13. How did you select the projects that you voted for?
14. Have you engaged in PB in earlier years?
15. Have any of your preferred projects been selected in previous years?
16. [If yes] Have any of those projects been completely implemented?
17. How satisfied or dissatisfied are you with the PB project(s) for this year? In past years? Why?
18. What have we not discussed that you think is important for understanding the process of how PB decisions are made?

Appendix D: Expo and Voting Schedule Information

PB Expos:

Thursday, March 28

District 3—Johnson
6:30 pm @ Hudson Guild
441 W. 26th St (between 9th & 10th Ave.)

Saturday, March 30

District 2—Rivera
LES Girls Club
402 E 8th St
New York, NY 10009

District 26—Van Bramer
12:30–3 pm @ Sunnyside Community Services
43-31 39th St, LIC

Tuesday, April 2

District 39—Lander
6–9 pm @ Park Slope Library

D. Williams and D. Waisanen, *Real Money, Real Power?*,
https://doi.org/10.1007/978-3-030-59201-1

PB Voting:

Saturday, March 30

District 3—Johnson
11 am–5 pm @ Fulton Houses Tenants Assoc. Office
419A W. 17th St.

District 3—Johnson
11 am–5 pm @ Hudson Guild Elliott Center
441 W. 26th Street

District 3—Johnson
11 am–5 pm @ Greenwich House
27 Barrow Street
District 3—Johnson
11 am–5 pm @ The LGBT Center
208 West 13th St.

District 3—Johnson
11 am–5 pm @ Manhattan Plaza
400 West 43rd Street & 484 West 43rd Street

District 8—Ayala
8 am–3 pm @ Manhattan Center for Science and Mathematics
280 Pleasant Ave.

District 8—Ayala
12 pm–5 pm @ Abraham House
340 Willis Avenue

District 22—Constantinides
12–4 pm @ Astoria Library
14-01 Astoria Blvd.

District 26—Van Bramer
12:30–3 pm @ Sunnyside Community Services
43-31 39th St, LIC

District 27—Miller
10 am–5 pm @ District Office
172-12 Linden Blvd

Sunday, March 31

District 3—Johnson
11 am–5 pm @ Fulton Houses Tenants Assoc. Office
419A W. 17th St.

District 3—Johnson
11 am–5 pm @ Hudson Guild Elliott Center
441 W. 26th Street

District 3—Johnson
11 am–5 pm @ Greenwich House
27 Barrow Street

District 3—Johnson
11 am–5 pm @ The LGBT Center
208 West 13th St.

District 3—Johnson
11 am–5 pm @ Manhattan Plaza
400 West 43rd Street & 484 West 43rd Street

District 3—Johnson
11 am–5 pm @ Penn South Community Room
343 8th Avenue (8A Community Room)

District 8—Ayala
8 am–3 pm @ Manhattan Center for Science and Mathematics
280 Pleasant Ave.

District 22—Constantinides
12–4 pm@ Urban Upbound
4-25 Astoria Blvd.

Monday April 1

District 3—Johnson
10 am–6 pm @ District Office
224 West 30th Street, Suite #1206

District 8—Ayala
8 am–3 pm @ Manhattan Center for Science and Mathematics
280 Pleasant Ave.

District 8—Ayala
9 am–6 pm @ District Office (East Harlem)
105 E. 116th St.

District 8—Ayala
9 am–5 pm @ District Office (South Bronx)
214 St. Ann's Ave.

District 8—Ayala
4 pm–6 pm @ Heketi Community Charter School
403 Concord Ave.

District 8—Ayala
2 pm–8 pm @ Taft Houses
1730 Madison Ave.

District 22—Constantinides
9 am–5 pm @ District Office
31-09 Newtown Ave., 209

District 26—Van Bramer
5–7 pm @ Queens Library (Court Square)
25-01 Jackson Ave.

District 26—Van Bramer
5:30–7:30 pm @ Jacob Riis Settlement
10-25 41st Ave.

District 27—Miller
10 am–5 pm @ District Office
172-12 Linden Blvd

District 27—Miller
2:30–5:30 pm @ Cambria Heights Library
218-13 Linden Blvd

District 27—Miller
3–5 pm @ St Albans Library
191-05 Linden Blvd.

District 39—Lander
District Office of Brad Lander
456 5th Ave., 3rd Floor

Tuesday, April 2

District 3—Johnson
10 am–6 pm @ District Office
224 West 30th Street, Suite #1206

District 8—Ayala
8 am–3 pm @ Manhattan Center for Science and Mathematics
280 Pleasant Ave.

District 8—Ayala
9 am–6 pm @ District Office (East Harlem)
105 E. 116th St.

District 8—Ayala
9 am–5 pm @ District Office (South Bronx)
214 St. Ann's Ave.

District 8—Ayala
9 am–5 pm @ Johnson Houses Community Center
1833 Lexington Ave.

District 8—Ayala
9:30 am–8 pm @ Bridge Builders
156 W. 164th St.

District 22—Constantinides
9 am–5 pm @ District Office
31-09 Newtown Ave., 209

District 26—Van Bramer
4–6 pm @ Queens Library (LIC)
37-44 21st St.

District 27—Miller
10 am–5 pm @ District Office
172-12 Linden Blvd

District 39—Lander
District Office of Brad Lander
456 5th Ave., 3rd Floor

Wednesday, April 3

District 3—Johnson
10 am–6 pm @ District Office
224 West 30th Street, Suite #1206

District 8—Ayala
8 am–3 pm @ Manhattan Center for Science and Mathematics
280 Pleasant Ave.

District 8—Ayala
9 am–6 pm @ District Office (East Harlem)
105 E. 116th St.

District 8—Ayala
9 am–5 pm @ District Office (South Bronx)
214 St. Ann's Ave.

District 8—Ayala
2:30 pm–6 pm @ Heketi Community Charter School
403 Concord Ave.

District 8—Ayala
2 pm–8 pm @ Taft Houses
1730 Madison Ave.

District 22—Constantinides
9 am–5 pm @ District Office
31-09 Newtown Ave., 209

District 26—Van Bramer
4–6 pm @ Queens Library (Broadway)
40-20 Broadway

District 26—Van Bramer
5:30–7:30 pm @ Woodside Houses Community Center

District 27—Miller
10 am–5 pm @ District Office
172-12 Linden Blvd

District 27—Miller
1:30–3 pm @ Alpha Phi Alpha Senior Center
220-01 Linden Blvd.

District 39—Lander
District Office of Brad Lander
456 5th Ave., 3rd Floor

Thursday, April 4

District 3—Johnson
10 am–6 pm @ District Office
224 West 30th Street, Suite #1206

District 8—Ayala
8 am–3 pm @ Manhattan Center for Science and Mathematics
280 Pleasant Ave.

District 8—Ayala
9 am–6 pm @ District Office (East Harlem)
105 E. 116th St.

District 8—Ayala
9 am–5 pm @ District Office (South Bronx)
214 St. Ann's Ave.

District 8—Ayala
2 pm–8 pm @ Taft Houses
1730 Madison Ave.

District 8—Ayala
Dream Charter School
232 E. 103rd St.

District 22—Constantinides
9 am–5 pm @ District Office
31-09 Newtown Ave., 209

District 22—Constantinides
6–8 pm @ Astoria Houses Community Center 4-05 Astoria Blvd

District 26—Van Bramer
5:30–7:30 pm @ Queens Library (Sunnyside)
43-06 Greenpoint Ave.

District 26—Van Bramer
5:30–7:30 pm @ Queens Library (Woodside)
54-22 Skillman Ave.

District 27—Miller
10 am–5 pm @ District Office
172-12 Linden Blvd

District 27—Miller
2–5 pm @ South Hollis Library
204-01 Hollis Ave.

District 27—Miller
3–6 pm @ Cambria Center for the Gifted Child,
233-10 Linden Blvd

District 27—Miller
3–6 pm @ South Jamaica Library
108-41 Guy R Brewer Blvd.

District 39—Lander
District Office of Brad Lander
456 5th Ave., 3rd Floor

District 6—Rosenthal
Broadway Mall Community Center 96th Street & Broadway,
April 4, 2019, 8:00–10:00 am

District 6—Rosenthal
Peter Jay Sharp Symphony Space 2537 Broadway,
April 4, 2019, 4:00–6:00 pm

Friday, April 5

District 3—Johnson
10 am–6 pm @ District Office
224 West 30th Street, Suite #1206

District 8—Ayala
8 am–3 pm @ Manhattan Center for Science and Mathematics
280 Pleasant Ave.

District 8—Ayala
9 am–6 pm @ District Office (East Harlem)
105 E. 116th St.

District 8—Ayala
9 am–5 pm @ District Office (South Bronx)
214 St. Ann's Ave.

District 8—Ayala
9 am–5 pm @ Johnson Houses Community Center
1833 Lexington Ave.

District 22—Constantinides
9 am–5 pm @ District Office
31-09 Newtown Ave., 209

District 27—Miller
10 am–5 pm @ District Office
172-12 Linden Blvd

District 39—Lander
District Office of Brad Lander
456 5th Ave., 3rd Floor

District 43—Brannan
10 am–5 pm @ 2213 Bath Avenue (Community Board 11)

Saturday, April 6

District 3—Johnson
11 am–5 pm @ Fulton Houses Tenants Assoc. Office
419A W. 17th St.

District 3—Johnson
11 am–5 pm @ Hudson Guild Elliott Center
441 W. 26th Street

District 3—Johnson
11 am–5 pm @ Greenwich House
27 Barrow Street

District 3—Johnson
11 am–5 pm @ The LGBT Center
208 West 13th St.

District 3—Johnson
11 am–5 pm @ Manhattan Plaza
400 West 43rd Street & 484 West 43rd Street

District 3—Johnson
11 am–5 pm @ Penn South Community Room
343 8th Avenue (8A Community Room)

District 8—Ayala
8 am–3 pm @ Manhattan Center for Science and Mathematics
280 Pleasant Ave.

District 8—Ayala
12–5 pm @ Abraham House
340 Willis Avenue

District 22—Constantinides
12–4 pm @ Astoria Library
14-01 Astoria Blvd.

District 27—Miller
10 am–5 pm @ District Office
172-12 Linden Blvd

District 35—Cumbo
10 am–2 pm @ Prospect Heights campus of BK Academy of Science and the Environment

District 35—Cumbo
10 am–2 pm @ Grand Army Plaza Greenmarket

District 35—Cumbo
8 am–3 pm @ Ft. Greene Park Artisan Market

District 39—Lander
10 am–4 pm @ Carroll Park House

District 39—Lander
12–6 pm @ Park Slope Armory YMCA
361 15th St.

District 39—Lander
5–7 pm @ Brooklyn Museum

District 43—Brannan
11 am–5 pm @ Bay Ridge Library

District 43—Brannan
11 am–4 pm @
District Office, 8018 5th Avenue, Brooklyn

Sunday, April 7

District 6—Rosenthal
Community Board 7 Office
250 W. 87th Street
12:00–2:00 pm

District 3—Johnson
11 am–5 pm @ Fulton Houses Tenants Assoc. Office
419A W. 17th St.

District 3—Johnson
11 am–5 pm @ Hudson Guild Elliott Center
441 W. 26th Street

District 3—Johnson
11 am–5 pm @ Greenwich House
27 Barrow Street

District 3—Johnson
11 am–5 pm @ The LGBT Center
208 West 13th St.

District 3—Johnson
11 am–5 pm @ Manhattan Plaza
400 West 43rd Street & 484 West 43rd Street

District 3—Johnson
11 am–5 pm @ Penn South Community Room
343 8th Avenue (8A Community Room)

District 8—Ayala
8 am–3 pm @ Manhattan Center for Science and Mathematics
280 Pleasant Ave.

District 26—Van Bramer
10 am–2 pm @ Queen of Angels Church
44-04 Skillman Ave.

District 35—Cumbo
10 am–2 pm @ Franklin Ave. subway stop

District 39—Lander
10 am–4 pm @ PS 230
425 MacDonald Ave.

District 39—Lander
10 am–4 pm @ Old Stone House
Washington Park, 336 3rd St.

References

Alves, M. H. M. (1990, September). Building democratic socialism: The Partido Dos Trabalhadores in Brazil. *Monthly Review, 42,* 1+ (Online).

Alves, M. L., & Allegretti, G. (2012). (In)stability, a key element to understand participatory budgeting: Discussing Portuguese cases. *Journal of Public Deliberation, 8*(2), Article 3.

Arnstein, S. R. (1969). A ladder of citizen participation. *Journal of the American Institute of Planners, 35*(4), 216–224.

Assies, W. (1993). Urban social movements and local democracy in Brazil. *Revista Europea de Estudios Latinoamericanos y del Caribe/European Review of Latin American and Caribbean Studies* (55), 39–58.

Avritzer, L. (2010). Living under a democracy: Participation and its impact on the living conditions of the poor. *Latin American Research Review, 45,* 166–185.

Baiocchi, G., & Ganuza, E. (2014). Participatory budgeting as if emancipation mattered. *Politics & Society, 42*(1), 29–50. https://doi.org/10.1177/0032329213512978.

Board of Estimate of NYC v. Morris, 489 U.S. 688 (1989).

Bremner, L. (1998). Participatory planning. *Urban Forum, 9*(1), 111–119.

Calabrese, T., Williams, D. W., & Gupta, A. (2020). Does participatory budgeting alter public spending? Evidence from New York City. *Administration and Society, 52*(9), 1382–1409. https://doi.org/10.1177/0095399720912548.

Castillo, M. (2015). Reflections on participatory budgeting in New York City. *The Innovation Journal: The Public Sector Innovation Journal, 20*(2), 1–11.

D. Williams and D. Waisanen, *Real Money, Real Power?*,
https://doi.org/10.1007/978-3-030-59201-1

de Sousa Santos, B. (1998). Participatory budgeting in Porto Alegre: Toward a redistributive democracy. *Politics and Society, 26*(4), 461–510.

Dyck, J. J., & Lascher, E. L. (2019). *Initiatives without engagement: A realistic appraisal of direct democracy's secondary effects*. Ann Arbor: University of Michigan Press.

Egan, S. (2016, May 19). Participatory budgeting funds new trees, cool Breezes. *The Villager*. Retrieved from https://www.thevillager.com/2016/05/participatory-budgeting-funds-new-trees-cool-breezes/.

Fung, A. (2006). Varieties of participation in complex governance. *Public Administration Review, 66*, 66–75.

Fung, A. (2015). Putting the public back into governance: The challenges of citizen participation and its future. *Public Administration Review, 75*(4), 513–522. https://doi.org/10.1111/puar.12361.

Fung, A., & Wright, E. O. (2001). Deepening democracy: Innovations in empowered participatory governance. *Politics & Society, 29*(1), 5–41.

Gelfand, A. (2016, November 25). Participatory budget community meeting. *The Wave*. Retrieved from https://www.rockawave.com/articles/participatory-budget-community-meeting/.

Gilman, H. R. (2012). Transformative deliberations: Participatory budgeting in the United States. *Journal of Public Deliberation, 8*(2) (Online).

Gilman, H. R. (2016). *Engaging citizens: Participatory budgeting and the inclusive governance movement within the United States*. Retrieved from http://ash.harvard.edu/files/ash/files/participatory-budgeting-paper.pdf?m=1455295224.

Goldfrank, B. (2007). Lessons from Latin American experience in participatory budgeting. In A. Shah (Ed.), *Participatory budgeting* (Vol. 143, pp. 91–126). Washington, DC: The World Bank.

Goldfrank, B. (2012). The World Bank and the globalization of participatory budgeting. *Journal of Public Deliberation, 8*(2), Article 7.

Goodsell, C. T. (2004). *The case for bureaucracy: A public administration polemic* (4th ed.). Washington, DC: CQ Press.

Guarino, D. (2015, October 9). Full plate at Rockaway Beach Civic. *The Wave*. Retrieved from https://www.rockawave.com/articles/full-plate-at-rockaway-beach-civic/.

Hadden, M., & Lerner, J. (2011, December 7). *How to start participatory budgeting in Your City*. Retrieved from http://www.commondreams.org/views/2011/12/07/how-start-participatory-budgeting-your-city.

Hagelskamp, C., Rinehart, C., Silliman, R., & Schleifer, D. (2016). *Why let the people decide? Elected officials on participatory budgeting*. Retrieved from https://www.publicagenda.org/files/WhyLetThePeopleDecide_PublicAgenda_2016.pdf.

Handbook for Community Board Members. (2014). In New York City (Ed.): Office of the Mayor Community Affairs Unit.

Hanrahan, L. (2019, March 25). Cast your ballot in the district 33 participatory budgeting vote next week. *Greenpoint Post*. Retrieved from https://greenpointpost.com/cast-your-ballot-in-the-district-33-participatory-budgeting-vote-next-week.

Hart, D. K. (1972). Theories of government related to decentralization and citizen participation. *Public Administration Review, 32*, 603–621. https://doi.org/10.2307/975228.

Hendy, J., & Barlow, J. (2012). The role of the organizational champion in achieving health system change. *Social Science & Medicine, 74*(3), 348–355.

Kasdan, A., & Cattell, L. (2012a). *A people's budget: A research and evaluation report on the pilot year of participatory budgeting in New York City*. Retrieved from https://cdp.urbanjustice.org/sites/default/files/pbreport.pdf.

Kasdan, A., & Cattell, L. (2012b). *A people's budget: A research and evaluation report on the pilot year of participatory budgeting in New York City*. Retrieved from https://www.issuelab.org/resource/a-people-s-budget-a-research-and-evaluation-report-on-the-pilot-year-of-participatory-budgeting-in-new-york-city.html.

Kasdan, A., & Markman, E. (2017). Participatory budgeting and community-based research: Principles, practices, and implications for impact validity. *New Political Science, 39*(1), 143–155.

Kasdan, A., Cattell, L., & Convey, P. (2013). *A people's budget: A research and evaluation report on participatory budgeting in New York City—Year 2*. Retrieved from https://cdp.urbanjustice.org/sites/default/files/pbreport_year2_0.pdf.

Kasdan, A., Markman, E., & Convey, P. (2014). *A people's budget: A research and evaluation report on participatory budgeting in New York City—Year 3*. Retrieved from https://cdp.urbanjustice.org/sites/default/files/CDP.WEB.doc_Report_PBNYC-cycle3-FullReport_20141030.pdf.

Kihss, P. (1963, April 29). New city charter still under test: Changes are numerous as system is learned. *The New York Times*, p. 23.

Lerner, J. (2011). Participatory budgeting: Building community agreement around tough budget decisions. *National Civic Review, 100*(2), 30–35. https://doi.org/10.1002/ncr.20059.

Macpherson, C. B. (1980). Pluralism, individualism, and participation. *Economic and Industrial Democracy, 1*(1), 21–30.

Maxey, C. C. (1919). A little history of pork. *National Municipal Review, 8*(10), 691–705. https://doi.org/10.1002/ncr.4110081006.

Mayorga, E. (2014). Toward digital, critical, participatory action research: Lessons from the #BarrioEdProj. *The Journal of Interactive Technology &*

Pedagogy, 5, 1–25. https://jitp.commons.gc.cuny.edu/toward-digital-critical-participatory-action-research/.
McCombs, M. E., & Shaw, D. L. (1993). The evolution of agenda-setting research: Twenty-five years in the marketplace of ideas. *Journal of Communication, 43*(2), 58–67.
McTigue, C., Rye, T., & Monios, J. (2018). The role of reporting mechanisms in transport policy implementation by local authorities in England. *Case Studies on Transport Policy, 6*(3), 319–328.
New York City. (2017). *Adopted Capital Budget For Fiscal Year 2018*. Retrieved from http://www1.nyc.gov/site/omb/publications/finplan06-17.page.
New York City Charter As Amended Through July 2004. (2004). Retrieved from www.nyc.gov/html/records/pdf/section%201133_citycharter.pdf accessible at http://www.amlegal.com/codes/client/new-york-city_ny/.
New York City Council. (2017). Rulebook 2017–2018 New York City participatory budgeting. In New York City Council (Ed.).
New York City Council. (2020). *Participatory budgeting*. Retrieved from https://council.nyc.gov/pb/.
New York City Population by Community Districts. (2017). Retrieved from https://data.cityofnewyork.us/City-Government/New-York-City-Population-By-Community-Districts/xi7c-iiu2/data.
Osborne, D., & Gaebler, T. (1992). *Reinventing government: How the entrepreneurial spirit is transforming the public sector*. Reading, MA: Addison-Wesley.
Paixão Bretas, P. R. (1996). Participative budgeting in Belo Horizonte: Democratization and citizenship. *Environment and Urbanization, 8*(1), 213–222.
Pape, M., & Lerner, J. (2016). Budgeting for equity: How can participatory budgeting advance equity in the United States? *Journal of Public Deliberation, 12*(2), Article 9.
Participatory Budgeting in New York City. (2011). *2011–2012 Handbook*.
Participatory Budgeting Project. (2017). *Participatory Budgeting Project*. Retrieved from https://www.participatorybudgeting.org/.
Participatory Budgeting Project. (2018). *PB map & process list*. Retrieved from https://www.participatorybudgeting.org/pb-map/.
Pateman, C. (1970). *Participation and democratic theory*. Cambridge, UK: University Press.
Pateman, C. (1975). A contribution to the political theory of organizational democracy. *Administration & Society, 7*(1), 5–26.
Pateman, C. (2012). APSA presidential address: Participatory democracy revisited. *Perspectives on Politics, 10*(1), 7–19.
Patsias, C., Latendresse, A., & Bherer, L. (2013). Participatory democracy, decentralization and local governance: The Montreal Participatory Budget in the light of 'empowered participatory governance'. *International Journal*

of Urban and Regional Research, 37(6), 2214–2230. https://doi.org/10.1111/j.1468-2427.2012.01171.x.

Pecorella, R. F. (1986). Community input and the city budget: Geographically based budgeting in New York City. *Journal of Urban Affairs, 8*(1), 57–70.

Pecorella, R. F. (1988). Community empowerment revisited: Two decades of integrative reform. *State & Local Government Review, 20*(2), 72–78.

Pecorella, R. F. (1989). Community governance: A decade of experience. *Proceedings of the Academy of Political Science, 37*(3), 97–109. https://doi.org/10.2307/1173755.

Pecorella, R. F. (1994). *Community power in a postreform city: Politics in New York City*. Armonk: ME Sharpe.

Pin, L. (2017). Does participatory budgeting lead to local empowerment? The case of Chicago, IL. *Alternate Routes: A Journal of Critical Social Research, 28*.

Pinnington, E., Lerner, J., & Schugurensky, D. (2009). Participatory budgeting in North America: The case of Guelph, Canada. *Journal of Public Budgeting, Accounting & Financial Management, 21*(3), 454–481.

Plott, C. R., & Levine, M. E. (1978). A model of agenda influence on committee decisions. *The American Economic Review, 68*(1), 146–160.

Plunkitt, G. W., & Riordon, W. L. (1905). *Plunkitt of Tammany Hall: A series of very plain talks on very practical politics*. New York: McClure, Phillips & Co.

Pozen, D. E. (2019). Seeing transparency more clearly. *Public Administration Review*. https://doi.org/10.1111/puar.13137.

Pressman, J. L., & Wildavsky, A. B. (1973). *Implementation: How great expectations in Washington are dashed in Oakland; or, Why it's amazing that Federal programs work at all, this being a saga of the Economic Development Administration as told by two sympathetic observers who seek to build morals on a foundation of ruined hopes*. Berkeley: University of California Press.

Rack, Y. (2015, October 15). Have your say—Participatory budgeting is back. *The Villager*. Retrieved from https://www.thevillager.com/2015/10/have-your-say-participatory-budgeting-is-back/.

Register of Community Board Budget Requests for the Executive Budget Fiscal Year 2018. (2017). Retrieved from http://www1.nyc.gov/assets/omb/downloads/pdf/cbrboro4-17.pdf.

Richard, E., & David, L. F. (2018). The future of citizen engagement in cities—The council of citizen engagement in sustainable urban strategies (ConCensus). *Futures, 101*, 80–91. https://doi.org/10.1016/j.futures.2018.06.012.

Robinson, A. (2011, November 13). How to spend a million bucks. *Mott Haven Herald*. Retrieved from http://www.motthavenherald.com/2011/11/13/how-to-spend-a-million-bucks/.

Rom, G. (2016, January 29). Participatory budgeting hits a roadblock in Queens. *TimesLedger*. Retrieved from https://www.timesledger.com/stories/2016/5/pbarticle_2016_01_29_q.html.

Shybalkina, I. (2019). Designing citizen participation processes to help people make more reasoned choices. In I. Shybalkina (Ed.), *Engagement-equity trade-off: A mixed-methods study of participatory budgeting and property tax assessment appeals in large US cities* (Dissertation). Draft chapter with shared info.

Shybalkina, I., & Bifulco, R. (2019). Does participatory budgeting change the share of public funding to low income neighborhoods? *Public Budgeting & Finance, 39*(1), 45–66. https://doi.org/10.1111/pbaf.12212.

Sintomer, Y., Herzberg, C., Allegretti, G., Röcke, A., & Alves, M. L. (2013). *Participatory budgeting worldwide.* Retrieved from https://estudogeral.sib.uc.pt/jspui/bitstream/10316/42267/1/Participatory%20Budgeting%20Worldwide.pdf.

Souza, C. (2001). Participatory budgeting in Brazilian cities: Limits and possibilities in building democratic institutions. *Environment and Urbanization, 13*(1), 159–184. https://doi.org/10.1177/095624780101300112.

Stone, C. N. (1980). Systemic power in community decision making: A restatement of stratification theory. *American Political Science Review, 74*(4), 978–990.

Su, C. (2012). Whose budget? Our budget? Broadening political stakeholdership via participatory budgeting. *Journal of Public Deliberation, 8*(2), Article 1.

Su, C. (2017a). *Beyond inclusion: Critical race theory and participatory budgeting*. CUNY Academic Works. Retrieved from http://academicworks.cuny.edu/gc_pubs/299.

Su, C. (2017b). *From Porto Alegre to New York City: Participatory budgeting and democracy.* CUNY Academic Works. City University of New York (CUNY). Retrieved from http://academicworks.cuny.edu/gc_pubs/305.

Su, C. (2018). Managed participation: City agencies and micropolitics in participatory budgeting. *Nonprofit and Voluntary Sector Quarterly, 47*(4_Suppl.), 76S–96S. https://doi.org/10.1177/0899764018757029.

Urban Justice Center. (2015). *A people's budget: A research and evaluation report on participatory budgeting in New York City—Cycle 4 key research findings.* Retrieved from https://cdp.urbanjustice.org/sites/default/files/CDP.WEB.doc_Report_PBNYC_cycle4findings_20151021.pdf.

Van Duyn, Emily. (2018). Hidden democracy: Political dissent in rural America. *Journal of Communication, 68*(5), 965–987.

Venugopal, N. (2016, March 25, 28). Here's how you can vote for Brooklyn School Diversity or Book-Drop Boxes. *DNA Info: Cobble Hill, Carroll Gardens & Red Hook* (Online).

Waisanen, D. (2012). Bordering populism in immigration activism: Outlaw–civic discourse in a (counter) public. *Communication Monographs, 79,* 232–255.

Waisanen, D. (2014). Toward robust public engagement: The value of deliberative discourse for civil communication. *Rhetoric & Public Affairs, 17,* 287–322.

Waisanen, D. (2018). *Political conversion: Personal transformation as strategic public communication.* Lexington Studies in Political Communication. Lanham, MD: Rowman & Littlefield.

Waisanen, D. (2020). *Improv for democracy: How to bridge differences and develop the communication and leadership skills our world needs.* New Political Science Series. Albany, NY: State University of New York Press.

Walker, J. L. (1977). Setting the agenda in the US Senate: A theory of problem selection. *British Journal of Political Science, 7*(4), 423–445.

Wampler, B. (2012). Participatory budgeting: Core principles and key impacts. *Journal of Public Deliberation, 8*(2), Article 12.

Wampler, B., & Avritzer, L. (2004). Participatory publics: Civil society and new institutions in democratic Brazil. *Comparative Politics, 36*(3), 291–312. https://doi.org/10.2307/4150132.

Wampler, B., & Touchton, M. (2016). Public engagement for public health: Participatory budgeting and infant mortality in Brazilian municipalities. In W. No, A. Brennan, & D. Schugurensky (Eds.), *By the people* (pp. 144–154). Phoenix, AZ: Arizona State University.

Wampler, B., McNulty, S., & Touchton, M. (2018). *Participatory budgeting: Spreading across the globe.* Retrieved from http://www.transparency-initiative.org/wp-content/uploads/2018/03/spreading-pb-across-the-globe_jan-2018.pdf.

Wan, P. Y.-Z. (2018). Outsourcing participatory democracy: Critical reflections on the participatory budgeting experiences in Taiwan. *Journal of Public Deliberation, 14*(1), 7.

Whitman, E. (2012, April 16). Participatory budgeting hits New York City. *The Nation* (Online).

Williams, D. W., Calabrese, T., Gupta, A., & Harju, S. (2017). *How does participatory budgeting affect council member priorities?* Paper presented at the Association of Budgeting & Financial Management Annual Conference, Washington.

Williams, Z. (2015a, May 14). Chelsea parks, Village library loo are big winners in participatory budgeting. *The Villager*. Retrieved from https://www.thevillager.com/2015/05/chelsea-parks-village-library-loo-are-big-winners-in-participatory-budgeting/.

Williams, Z. (2015b, April 2). Local projects want your vote! $1M up for grabs. *The Villager*. Retrieved from https://www.thevillager.com/2015/04/local-projects-want-your-vote-1m-up-for-grabs/.

Wolfe, J. D. (1985). A defense of participatory democracy. *The Review of Politics, 47*(3), 370–389.

Wong, P. (2018, May 1). District 39 participatory budgeting 2018: Winning projects announced. *Bklyner* (Online). Retrieved from https://bklyner.com/district-39-participatory-budgeting-2018-winning-projects-announced/.

Index

D. Williams and D. Waisanen, *Real Money, Real Power?*,
https://doi.org/10.1007/978-3-030-59201-1

The manufacturer's authorised representative in the EU is Springer Nature Customer Service Centre GmbH, Europaplatz 3, 69115 Heidelberg, Germany. If you have any concerns regarding our products, please contact ProductSafety@springernature.com

Printed and bound by CPI Group (UK) Ltd, Croydon, CR0 4YY
30/09/2026
02225466-0003